MW00737058

VISUAL QUICKSTART GUIDE

QUICKEN 2000

FOR MACINTOSH

Tom Negrino

Peachpit Press

Visual QuickStart Guide
Quicken 2000 for Macintosh
Tom Negrino

Peachpit Press
1249 Eighth Street
Berkeley, CA 94710
510/524-2178
800/283-9444
510/524-2221 fax

Find us on the World Wide Web at: http://www.peachpit.com

Peachpit Press is a division of Addison Wesley Longman

Copyright © 1999 Tom Negrino

Editor: Lisa Theobald
Production Coordinator: Mimi Heft
Cover design: The Visual Group
Compositor: David Van Ness
Indexer: Karin Arrigoni

Notice of rights
All rights reserved. No part of this book may be reproduced or transmitted in any form by any means, electronic, mechanical, photocopying, recording, or otherwise, without the prior written permission of the publisher. For information on getting permission for reprints and excerpts, contact Gary-Paul Prince at Peachpit Press.

Notice of liability
The information in this book is distributed on an "As Is" basis, without warranty. While every precaution has been taken in the preparation of the book, neither the author nor Peachpit Press, shall have any liability to any person or entity with respect to any loss or damage caused or alleged to be caused directly or indirectly by the instructions contained in this book or by the computer software and hardware products described in it.

Trademarks
Many of the designations used by manufacturers and sellers to distinguish their products are claimed as trademarks. Where those designations appear in this book, and Peachpit Press was aware of a trademark claim, the designations appear as requested by the owner of the trademark. All other product names and services identified throughout this book are used in editorial fashion only and for the benefit of such companies. No such use, or the use of any trade name, is intended to convey endorsement or other affiliation with the book.

Quicken, QuickBooks, and MacInTax are registered trademarks of Intuit, Inc. Quicken.com is a trademark of Intuit, Inc.

ISBN 0-201-69964-8

0 9 8 7 6 5 4 3 2 1

Printed and bound in the United States of America

♻ Printed on recycled paper

Dedication

To my father Joseph Negrino, who has touched so many people's lives, becoming more than their accountant; he's become their friend. Thanks for the inspiration, Dad.

Special Thanks to:

Tom Baer, for all of his work.

The folks at Peachpit:

My editor, Lisa Theobald, for shepherding the book through even when things got difficult.

Mimi Heft, for her production wizardry, and for taming Microsoft Word's templates.

Nancy Ruenzel and Marjorie Baer, for believing in the project.

The people at Intuit:

Kelly O'Neil, the lady with the answers.

Adam Samuels, who got behind and pushed when necessary.

I'd also like to thank my agent, StudioB's David Rogelberg, and Sherry Rogelberg, AKA The Check Goddess.

Thanks to Sean Smith, for remaining the World's Best Kid™.

Thanks always to Dori Smith, for her love, smart advice, and incredible support. You've made my dreams come true.

TABLE OF CONTENTS

Chapter 3: **Tracking with Categories**   **21**

Chapter 4: **Using the Account Registers**   **31**

Chapter 5: **All About QuickFill**   **47**

INTRODUCTION

Money pervades our lives, simultaneously desired and disdained. Most of us can't get along without it and would love to have more of it. Yet many of us don't do an especially good job of managing the money that we do have. How often have you heard people say things like "I don't know where all my money goes"? Many people live from paycheck to paycheck, just getting along with no financial plan for the future and hardly any control over their financial present. In the meantime, they're building up consumer debt and digging themselves a hole that will take a long time to get out of.

Sound familiar? It certainly does to me; I was one of those people for many years. I finally got fed up with feeling that my finances were out of my control, so one December evening I bought a copy of Quicken Deluxe and promised myself that I would start using it when the new year began. Unlike some of my other New Year's resolutions, I did start using Quicken, and melodramatic as it sounds, it changed my life. I used Quicken to take stock of my finances and identify where I was handling my money poorly. Then I came up with a plan to pay off my debts and start saving for the future. I then kept track of my plan using Quicken's reports and graphs. Today I'm happy to say that I no longer wonder what my financial picture is, because Quicken gives me all the information that I need. There were some ups and downs, but I made it to fiscal sanity. So can you.

If you want to get better control over your finances, this book is for you. I'll show you how to use Quicken to help you get out of debt, manage your present finances, and invest for the future.

Welcome, iMac owners!

I'd especially like to welcome aboard owners of Apple's cool iMac computer. In fact, you folks are one of the main reasons this book was written; when I found out in 1998 that every iMac would include a copy of Quicken Deluxe, I suggested to my editors at Peachpit Press that iMac owners deserved a book about Quicken that was as friendly as the iMac itself. I was sure that the iMac was going to be a hit. Luckily, they had the good sense to agree. With Quicken Deluxe 2000 shipping with iMacs beginning Fall 1999, it made sense to update the book for the new version, and for all those new iMac owners.

Just the facts, Ma'am

I have to admit that I don't have a lot of patience for computer books that are thick and heavy enough to cause injury if you accidentally drop them on your foot. I'd rather open a book, find out how to do a task, and toss the book back on the shelf without wading through endless blather and more details than I ever wanted to know.

In this book, I've organized different financial tasks into chapters, and within each chapter are step-by-step directions that tell you exactly how to accomplish various tasks.

My assumptions about you

In writing this book, I've made the following assumptions about you. First, you own Quicken Deluxe 2000 and a Macintosh powerful enough to run the program. That's not a difficult requirement, as Quicken 2000 will run on any machine using a Power PC processor, with at least 32 of RAM, running Mac OS 8.1 or higher. That pretty much means that if your Macintosh was built anytime after about 1994, and you've been reasonably diligent in upgrading the Mac OS system software, chances are it will run Quicken just fine.

I've also made the assumption that you're familiar with the basics of using a Macintosh. You don't need be a Mac guru, although you shouldn't be stumped by concepts like selecting text, clicking and dragging, and using files and folders. If you need to brush up on the essentials, allow me to suggest that you pick up a copy of the excellent *Mac OS 8.6: Visual QuickStart Guide*, by Maria Langer, coincidentally also published by Peachpit Press.

Last, I've made the assumption that if you have bought this book, you're a person of uncommon discernment, style, and grace. If you're just leafing through these pages in a bookstore, I'm trusting you not to let me down.

What's not in this book

Because I wanted to write a book that was genuinely useful, rather than one that slavishly touched every base and documented every Quicken feature, I had to decide what I didn't want to put in the book. So I looked through Quicken for features that were little used or that weren't that great. The first feature to get the heave-ho was Budgeting. Making budgets is one of those things that everyone says they want to do, but hardly anyone really does. This isn't just my opinion; I've seen surveys of real Quicken users that bear me out. My apologies to you if you are one of the few, the proud, who really do budgets. A close relative to Budgeting is Forecasting, which also did not make the cut.

While I've included two chapters on investments, those chapters are intended for the relatively light-duty investor. If you have a modest stock portfolio, some mutual funds, and some other savings plans, the investment chapters should work just fine for you. But it you're constantly churning your portfolio, buying and selling options, and otherwise serious about playing the markets, you might find my investment chapters to be a bit thin.

I've also skipped over some of the less-interesting of Quicken's companion programs, such as the Refinance calculator and the Quicken Home Inventory program, the latter of which is one of the few outright flops in the otherwise-excellent Quicken package.

Let's get started

A popular bit of philosophy states that "The journey is the reward." I'm afraid that my pragmatic side says that when it comes to money, I believe that "The reward is the reward." In this case, the reward of using Quicken can mean smarter control over your finances, and in turn a better and richer life for yourself and for your family. That's a journey well worth taking. Thanks for joining me.

Tom Negrino

August 1999

INTRODUCING QUICKEN 2000

1

Welcome to Quicken 2000! In this chapter, you'll learn how to install and start Quicken, convert old Quicken files (if you've been using an older version of the program), use Quicken's interface, ask Quicken for help, and customize Quicken so that it works the way you do.

Installing and Running Quicken the First Time

Like most programs these days, Quicken provides step-by-step instructions for installation as soon as you load the product's CD-ROM. In case you need a little extra information, here's a bit of guidance to help you get the application up and running on your computer.

To install Quicken 2000:

1. Insert the Quicken CD-ROM in your CD-ROM drive. Double-click the Quicken icon (**Figure 1.1**) in the Quicken 2000 or Quicken 2000 Deluxe CD window that opens on your desktop.

2. The first screens that open deal with things like the license to use the software. Read them if you like; otherwise, keep clicking Agree, Continue, or Next until you get to the Install window.

3. Choose the Easy Install option (that's what most people do) (**Figure 1.2**). Click the Install button and Quicken will automatically finish installing the program. If you wish to, choose a location for the Quicken folder. By default, it will be put on the top level of your hard drive.

Double-click to Quicken 2000

Figure 1.1 The installation process begins when you double-click the Quicken icon.

Figure 1.2 Most people choose the Easy Install option.

Installing and Running Quicken

Quicken Deluxe 2000

Figure 1.3 Clicking on the program icon in the Quicken folder launches Quicken.

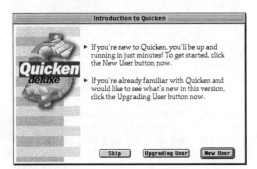

Figure 1.4 When you open Quicken the first time, you can use the tutorial to lead you through setting up a data file.

To launch Quicken 2000 the first time:

1. Double-click the Quicken folder on your hard disk to open it.

2. Double-click the Quicken Deluxe 2000 or the Quicken 2000 icon in the Quicken folder (**Figure 1.3**).

3. When Quicken asks you to personalize your copy, type in your name.

   Quicken then offers a quick tutorial to help either new users or upgrading users (**Figure 1.4**). In the tutorial, users are guided step by step through the process of setting up a data file.

INSTALLING AND RUNNING QUICKEN

To convert old Quicken files:

1. Choose File > Open File. The Open file dialog appears (**Figure 1.5**).

2. Navigate to the old Quicken file, select it, and then click the Open button.

   Quicken converts your old file into the current version's format.

✔ Tip

■ The conversion process is irreversible, so be sure to save a backup copy of each older version Quicken file before you convert it to Quicken 2000. You might need to refer to it.

■ After Quicken 2000 has successfully converted your previous version data file, it's important that you remove old versions of the Quicken application from your hard disk. You won't want to accidentally open your Quicken 2000 file with an older version because it's possible to corrupt your data.

To quit Quicken:

◆ Choose File > Quit, or press ⌘Q.

   Quicken will close all open windows and return to the Finder. You don't have to worry about saving your work because Quicken automatically saves it for you.

Figure 1.5 Locate and convert Quicken 98 files in the Open File dialog box. Depending on what version of the Mac OS is installed on your machine, the Open file dialog may look different. That's OK.

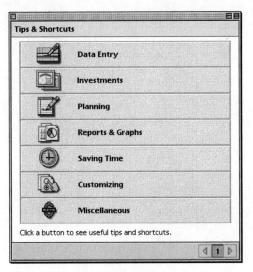

Figure 1.6 The Tips & Shortcuts window provides quick advice on a number of topics.

Activity Areas

Intuit has divided Quicken 2000 into five activity areas, each representing a different set of financial tasks:

◆ The **Banking** area lets you work with different bank accounts, including checking, savings, and money-market accounts.

◆ In the **Investing** area, you'll track stocks, bonds, mutual funds, and other investments in your portfolio.

◆ In the **Assets & Debt** section, you can deal with credit cards, loans, mortgages, and assets such as your home.

◆ **Planning** lets you budget and forecast your finances and figure out how to get out of debt, and its calculators can help you plan for your retirement.

◆ The **Reporting** area lets you create reports and graphs to show what's happening with your money.

✔ Tip

■ To see Tips at any time, choose Help > Tips & Shortcuts to open the Tips & Shortcuts window (**Figure 1.6**).

ACTIVITY AREAS

Finding Your Way Around

The Quicken 2000 program has a lot of features, and keeping track of them all can be a bit of a challenge. Let's start by taking a look at the Quicken window. At the top of the window is the standard Macintosh style menu bar, where you'll find Quicken's commands. But to make it all a little more "Intuit-ive," the main user interface is a set of tabs and buttons in the tool bar to present the various features at your disposal.

The menu bar

There isn't much to say about the menu bar (**Figure 1.7**) except that you can make any of its commands keyboard shortcuts. As with any Mac program, the commands Quicken needs to do your bidding are located on the menus.

The backdrop

To reduce confusion between Quicken's windows and windows in the Finder, Quicken hides the Finder and other applications behind a backdrop. If you want to get to the Finder, click in the dog-eared part of the backdrop at the lower right corner of the screen.

| File   Edit   Lists   Activities   Online   Help |

Figure 1.7 The menu bar is compact but has everything you need to put Quicken to work.

FINDING YOUR WAY AROUND

The tool bar

The tool bar (**Figure 1.8**) provides another way for you to choose Quicken commands. You can select a tab and display a set of command and account buttons that pertain to each activity area.

Each tab has a customizable set of buttons that, when clicked, initiate actions by Quicken. Some of these actions involve going online; their buttons have cute little lightning bolts on them.

Below the command buttons are the account buttons that, when clicked, open the registers of your various accounts.

Figure 1.8 The tool bar is divided into four areas.

Customizing Your Workspace

Quicken gives you a variety of ways to customize the program to your personal style. For example, you can put the functions you use all the time at your fingertips and hide those you don't need.

To change or eliminate the backdrop:

1. Choose Edit > Preferences, and then click the General icon (**Figure 1.9**).

2. To change the color of the backdrop, scroll in the horizontal color area near the bottom of the window, select a color by clicking it, and then click the OK button.

3. To eliminate the backdrop, clear the "Show backdrop behind windows" check box and then click the OK button.

Figure 1.9 The backdrop can be changed or removed in the Preferences dialog box.

Figure 1.10 The Configure Toolbar window box provides a high degree of customization of the user interface.

Figure 1.11 A tool bar that includes only the names of your account registers doesn't use a lot of valuable desktop real estate.

To customize the tool bar:

1. Choose Edit > Configure Toolbar to open the Configure Toolbar window that describes the buttons on the active tab (**Figure 1.10**). Then you can do any or all of the following:

   ◆ Drag command buttons from the Configure Toolbar window to the tool bar to install them, or drag buttons off the tool bar to remove them. Drag buttons around on the tool bar to rearrange them as you wish.

   ◆ Drag the names of your accounts to a tool bar to install account buttons, or remove buttons by dragging them off the tool bar.

   ◆ Create additional tabs by clicking the New Tab button and typing a name in the field in place of Tab field. Tabs can be removed by dragging them down from the tool bar to the Configure Toolbar dialog box.

   ◆ Hide either or both sets of buttons or the tabs themselves by checking or unchecking their respective boxes.

2. Repeat this for each of the tabs whose tool bars you want to customize. You can add the same buttons to several tool bars.

3. When you're finished customizing, click Change at the bottom of the Configure Toolbar window. Or you can choose Cancel to leave the tool bar as it was or choose Revert to Default Settings to take it back to square one.

✔ Tip

■ If you are using only a limited number of Quicken's functions, you may want to make more room on the desktop by unchecking the Show Tabs and Show Command Buttons boxes and leaving only a narrow bar with the account buttons at the top of the window (**Figure 1.11**).

CUSTOMIZING YOUR WORKSPACE

To create your own Command-key shortcuts:

1. Hold down the ⌘ key and click in the menu bar. The mouse cursor turns into the command symbol (**Figure 1.12**). Don't release the mouse button.

2. Let go of the ⌘ key and select the menu command to which you want to assign the shortcut.

3. With the command selected, release the mouse button. The Edit Command Key window appears (**Figure 1.13**) and shows you the name of the menu command and the existing shortcut (if one exists).

4. Type in the letter or symbol of the key that will be combined with the ⌘ key, and then click the OK button.

   If another menu command already uses the same shortcut key, Quicken will ask you to confirm your change. If you confirm, Quicken removes the shortcut from the other command and assigns the shortcut to the key you've selected.

To have Quicken automatically back up your data file:

1. Choose Edit > Preferences. The Preferences window appears.

2. In the scrolling area at the left edge of the Preferences window, scroll down and click the File Backup icon (**Figure 1.14**).

3. Click the "Automatically back up my data file when closing" check box.

4. Click the OK button.

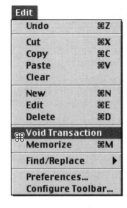

Figure 1.12 Hold down the ⌘ key while clicking a command to assign keyboard shortcuts to menu commands.

Figure 1.13 Assigning a keyboard command to a function can make your work much more efficient.

Figure 1.14 Quicken can be configured to automatically back up your data on a regular basis.

Figure 1.15 You can assign passwords to limit access to your files.

To protect your data file with a password:

1. Choose Edit > Preferences. The Preferences window appears.

2. In the scrolling area at the left edge of the window, scroll down and click the Passwords icon (**Figure 1.15**).

3. To require use of a password when opening a file, enter a password in the "To open a file" Password field.

4. To require use of a password when changing a transaction, enter a password in the "To modify transactions" Password field.

5. Click the OK button.

✔ Tip

■ **Warning!** If you later forget your password(s), the only way to get access to your data is to send your entire data file to Intuit. The company's crack team of code breakers will remove your passwords, but Intuit will also charge you a fee for the service.

Getting On-Screen Help

Quicken provides several options for on-screen help (although none are as wonderful as this book, naturally). Not surprisingly, you get to the program's help files via the Help menu (**Figure 1.16**).

About Quicken Help

Choose About Quicken Help to see an overview screen that shows you the different ways to get help (**Figure 1.17**). Click one of the buttons to find out more about that particular help option.

Balloon Help

Choose Show Balloons from the Help menu to turn on Balloon Help, which shows you descriptions of items when you point at them (**Figure 1.18**). Balloon Help is useful to help you learn about unfamiliar features, but you'll probably grow tired of the balloons popping up everywhere you move the mouse. To turn off Balloon Help, choose Hide Balloons from the Help menu.

Figure 1.16 The Help menu displays a range of help options.

Figure 1.17 This window gives an overview of the different help possibilities.

Figure 1.18 Balloon Help provides basic information in balloons that pop up on your screen.

GETTING ON-SCREEN HELP

Figure 1.19 The Quicken Help window has Topics, Index, and Search options.

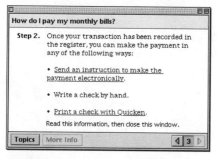

Figure 1.20 Quicken Help gives step-by-step instructions.

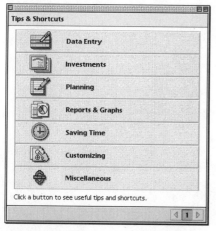

Figure 1.21 The Tips & Shortcuts window contains useful bits of knowledge.

Quicken Help

Quicken Help gives you step-by-step instructions on how to accomplish tasks. The Quicken Help window is divided into topic areas (**Figure 1.19**). You are then guided step by step through the procedure associated with the topic you choose (**Figure 1.20**), with hypertext links to related tasks. This is the best help tool to use for learning new tasks.

Tips & Shortcuts

These quick-tip topics (**Figure 1.21**) help you get more out of Quicken and show you how to accomplish tasks more quickly and easily.

User's Guide

Select this item to open the Quicken User's Guide in Adobe Acrobat format (**Figure 1.22**). The User's Guide is extensive and thoroughly indexed.

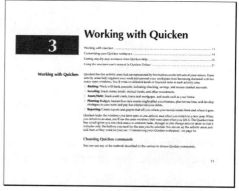

Figure 1.22 The User's Guide provides a thorough explanation of the Quicken program.

GETTING ON-SCREEN HELP

What Other Programs Come with Quicken Deluxe?

Quicken Deluxe 2000, which is bundled with the Apple iMac computer and also sold separately, includes these useful additions to the basic Quicken 2000 product:

- **QuickEntry** is a mini application that lets you enter transactions into any Quicken account without opening Quicken itself. For more on QuickEntry, see Chapter 4.

- The **Emergency Records Organizer** application saves your personal information in one place.

- The **Quicken Home Inventory** program helps you put together an inventory of your possessions.

- The **Tax Deduction Finder** steps you through a simple questionnaire that helps determine whether you might qualify for additional tax deductions.

- You can obtain a free copy of your **credit report**.

- The **Debt Reduction Planner** evaluates your debt level and steps you through creation of an action plan to get you out of debt faster.

- The **Retirement Planner** helps you create a plan to reach your retirement goals.

- In the **Net Worth Analysis**, you'll get a snapshot of your financial health.

- **Quicken Basics** are QuickTime tutorials that teach you about various Quicken tasks.

- The on-screen **User's Guide** in Adobe Acrobat format gives you quick answers.

SETTING UP ACCOUNTS

2

Quicken stores all of your information on your hard disk in a *data file* that you create the first time you use the program. You need only one data file, but inside the data file you'll create a number of accounts. An *account* represents an asset (something that you own, such as the money in your checking account or some property) or a liability (a debt that you owe, such as the balance on your credit cards or a mortgage).

Quicken allows you to have as many or as few accounts as you wish (actually, the upper limit is 255 accounts, but most people won't use more than a couple dozen accounts). Some people prefer to use Quicken to track only their main checking account, and other people create many accounts to track every penny.

In this chapter, you'll set up your data file and learn about the different account types within Quicken.

Creating a Data File

The first time you run Quicken, you'll need to create a data file to contain all your financial information. A data file must include at least one account, so you will create your checking account immediately after you create the data file.

To create a new data file and checking account:

1. Choose File > New File. The New File dialog box appears, asking if you're sure that you want to create a new data file (**Figure 2.1**). Click OK.

   The Save dialog box appears (**Figure 2.2**).

2. Navigate to where you want to save your data file, and enter a name for the file in the Name field.

   You can include Quicken's standard home or business categories in your data file. Categories are labels that you assign to your transactions that help you track where your money comes and goes.

3. Choose the Home or Business check box (or both), and then click the New button.

   The Set Up Account window appears (**Figure 2.3**).

Figure 2.1 Reassure Quicken that you indeed want to create a new file by clicking the OK button.

Figure 2.2 Choose where you want to save your data file and name it in the Save dialog box.

Figure 2.3 Create a new account in the Set Up Account window.

Figure 2.4 Quicken opens a register for the new account.

4. Click the Bank radio button. You use this radio button to set up checking, savings, or money-market accounts.

5. Enter a name for your checking account.

6. Enter a description for the checking account (optional).

7. Click the Create button.

   Quicken creates the account and opens a register for the new checking account (**Figure 2.4**), ready for you to enter the opening balance in the Deposit field.

8. Type the ending balance from your last bank statement into the Deposit field, and then press the [Tab] key until the Date field is highlighted. Type in the last statement date, and then click the Record button (or press the [Enter] key).

✔ Tip

■ Whenever you click the Record button, Quicken saves your work, so you don't need to worry about saving before you quit the program.

CREATING A DATA FILE

Using Accounts

Quicken has five kinds of accounts that you can use to track your assets:

- A **Bank** account tracks checking accounts, money-market accounts, savings accounts, and debit cards. This is the only account type you can use to make electronic payments or to write checks.

- An **Asset** account tracks the value of an asset, such as real estate or your car.

- The **Portfolio** account type tracks brokerage accounts that contain financial instruments, such as stocks and bonds.

- A **Mutual Fund** account tracks a single mutual fund.

- A **Cash** account is unlike the rest of the accounts because no corresponding account exists in a financial institution. You use a Cash account to track out-of-pocket expenses. For example, let's say that you withdraw $100 from an ATM. In Quicken, that amount comes out of your checking account and goes into the Cash account. As you spend the money, you can make notations in the Cash account to track how that cash has been spent.

Quicken also has two account types to track your liabilities:

- **Credit Card** accounts can track your credit cards, equity lines, and other lines of credit.

- **Liability** accounts are usually loans, such as a mortgage or car loan.

Figure 2.5 After you create a new account, it appears in the Accounts window.

To create a new account:

1. Choose Lists > Accounts to open the Accounts window (**Figure 2.5**).

2. Click New at the bottom of the Accounts window.

    The Set Up Account window appears (see **Figure 2.3**).

3. Select the radio button corresponding to the kind of account you wish to create, type in an account name, and enter a description (optional). Click the Create button.

    Quicken creates the account, adds its name to the Account list in the Accounts window, and opens its register.

4. Enter an opening balance, and if necessary change the date. See **Table 2.1** for guidance on which amounts and dates to use for opening balances.

Table 2.1

Entering Opening Balances

ACCOUNT TYPE	OPENING BALANCE	DATE
Bank	New balance from your last bank statement	Date of your last statement
Credit card	New balance from your last statement	Date of your last statement
Asset	The asset's current value	Today's date
Liability	The liability's current value	Today's date
Portfolio	See Chapter 15	
Mutual fund	See Chapter 15	
Cash	Current cash on hand	Today's date

USING ACCOUNTS

To edit or hide an account:

1. If the Accounts window is not already open, choose Lists > Accounts, or press ⌘Ⓐ.

2. Select an account and click the Edit button.

   The Edit Account window (**Figure 2.6**), which looks just like the Set Up Account window, appears.

3. Change the account information. If you no longer use an account and you don't want it cluttering up your Accounts window, you can hide it by clicking the "Hide in lists" check box in the Edit Account window. Then click the Change button.

To delete an account:

1. Choose Lists > Accounts, or press ⌘Ⓐ. The Accounts window appears.

2. Select an account, and then click the Delete button. Click the Yes button when Quicken asks you to confirm the account deletion (**Figure 2.7**).

✔ Tips

- Although you'll hardly ever need to delete an account, if you do, you lose the record of all the transactions that ever occurred in that account. Because this can mess up your reports, you're usually better off hiding an account rather than deleting it.

- If you need to see accounts that you've hidden, click the "Show hidden accounts" checkbox at the bottom of the Accounts window (refer to **Figure 2.5**).

Figure 2.6 The Edit Account window allows you to change account information and hide an account.

Figure 2.7 Quicken wants you to be sure that you really want to irreversibly delete an account.

TRACKING WITH CATEGORIES

3

The point of using Quicken is to gain better control over your finances. And to achieve that control, you'll need to know where your money comes from and where your money goes. You use Quicken's *categories* to track the flow of money. A category is simply a label that you assign to a transaction. For example, when you buy food at the grocery store and record the transaction in a Quicken register, you can record it under the category "Groceries." Later, when you're curious about how much money you spend on groceries, you can create a report that adds up all of your transactions for groceries.

By categorizing all of your transactions in Quicken, you can generate reports about the details of your income and expenses, save time and money while preparing your tax returns, and even set up budgets and compare what you're actually spending to what you had planned to spend.

Assigning Categories

Because categories are used to track the flow of money, you are naturally concerned about whether the money is flowing in or out. Money that is flowing in, such as your paycheck and investment income, is tracked using income categories. Money that you spend on your mortgage, utilities, groceries, entertainment, and other bills is tracked using expense categories.

You can—and should—assign a category to each transaction that you enter into Quicken. You should also use the same category names consistently throughout your Quicken accounts. For example, if you go to the doctor and pay with a check, you would enter that check under the "Medical" category in your checking account register. If on a subsequent visit you pay with a credit card, you would enter the transaction in your credit card account register using the category "Medical." This consistency is important: Consistent categorization leads to accurate reports.

✔ Tip

- When you created your data file (see Chapter 2), you probably included one of the preset categories lists, either the home categories or the business categories. You can use these category lists as is, but most people end up customizing their categories to better reflect their particular financial situations.

Figure 3.1 Click the New button in the Categories & Transfers window to create a new category.

Figure 3.2 Enter a name and description in the Set Up Category dialog box.

To create a new category:

1. Choose Lists > Categories & Transfers, or press ⌘L.

   The Categories & Transfers window appears (**Figure 3.1**).

2. At the bottom of the Categories & Transfers window, click the New button.

   The Set Up Category dialog box appears (**Figure 3.2**).

3. Enter a name for the category in the Category box.

4. Enter a description for the category in the Description box (optional).

5. Select the appropriate radio button for the new category type (Income or Expense).

6. Click the "Tax-related" check box if you want to use the category to track tax-related income or expenses.

7. Click the Create button.

   Quicken creates the category and adds it to the list in the Categories & Transfers window.

Assigning Subcategories

You'll often want to track several types of income or expenses that are related to a single category. Quicken allows you to use subcategories to handle these relations. For example, under the Medical category, you might have separate subcategories for Doctors, Dentists, Prescriptions, and Insurance. Later, when you run an expense report, you'll be able to see just how much money you've spent on each of the Medical subcategories.

To create a subcategory:

1. In the Categories & Transfers window, select a category for which you would like to create a subcategory.

2. Click the Add Subcategory button.

   The Set Up Category dialog box appears, but the Type radio buttons are dimmed (**Figure 3.3**). That's because a subcategory must always be of the same type as its parent category.

3. Enter the subcategory name in the Category box.

4. Enter the subcategory description in the Description box (optional).

5. If necessary, click the "Tax-related" check box.

6. Click the Create button.

   Quicken creates the subcategory, indenting it under the main category in the Categories & Transfers window (**Figure 3.4**).

Figure 3.3 Enter the subcategory name and description in this dialog box.

Figure 3.4 After you create a subcategory, Quicken adds its name to the Categories & Transfers window.

How Detailed Should I Get?

Quicken's preset categories are useful, but they're unlikely to completely satisfy your needs. No problem; just add more categories. But how much is enough?

The answer depends on the complexity of your financial picture and the level of detail to which you wish to track it. Here's an example. Robert is a salesman for a company and is constantly on the road. The company reimburses Robert for some of his auto expenses, so he tracks those expenses in great detail. Under his main Auto category, he has included subcategories for Maintenance, Fuel, Insurance, etc. Robert creates monthly Auto expense reports so that he can be reimbursed.

Susan works as an executive for the same corporation. She's curious to know how much she spends each year on her car. She doesn't care about the details; she just wants to know if her car expenses are growing or shrinking from year to year. So she uses one Auto category to track all expenses related to her car.

Your answer to the above question, then, depends on what kind of information is important to you. In general, you'll want to create subcategories for important elements so that you can track income or expenses in detail.

To edit a category or subcategory:

1. Select the category or subcategory in the Categories & Transfers window.

2. Click the Edit button.

   The Edit Category window appears. This window works in exactly the same way as the Set Up Category window, except that the button that accepts the changes you make is labeled Change, instead of Create.

3. Make your changes, and then click the Change button.

To delete a category or subcategory:

1. Select the category or subcategory in the Categories & Transfers window.

2. Click the Delete button. When Quicken asks you to confirm the deletion, click the Yes button.

ASSIGNING SUBCATEGORIES

Using Tax Links

Quicken makes it easy for you to create tax reports by marking a selected category as tax-related and then linking that category to a line item from a particular US federal tax form. Several of the preset categories are already assigned to tax forms; these are marked with a diamond character in the Categories & Transfers window.

To assign a tax link:

1. Select a category or subcategory in the Categories & Transfers window.

2. Click the Tax Links button.

   The Assign Tax Links window appears (**Figure 3.5**).

3. Scroll through the Line Item list, and select the appropriate line item. Then click the Assign button.

4. Click the Done button.

   Quicken links that line item to the category you selected in step 1.

✔ Tip

■ Tax Links are linked to individual lines (by description, not by line number) on the various US federal tax forms. These lines sometimes change from year to year as the tax laws (and therefore forms) change. Quicken 2000 is based on the 1998 tax year, so you should review your Tax Schedule report (see Chapter 16) to make sure that Quicken is categorizing Tax Links correctly for the 2000 and later tax years.

Figure 3.5 Select the appropriate line item from the list to assign the item to a category.

USING TAX LINKS

Using Classes

Classes are another way to group transactions. Classes do not replace categories; instead, a class adds an extra level to a transaction that has already been assigned to a category.

When you assign a category to a transaction, you can also assign a class to the transaction by adding a slash (/) followed by the class name to the end of the category name. For example, Bob's medical expenses could be categorized as Medical/Bob. This way, you can easily generate one report for the family's medical expenses (a category), another for Bob's expenses in general (a class), and another for Bob's medical expenses (sorting for both class and category).

Use classes to help you avoid unnecessary subcategories. In the example above, it's possible (although inefficient) to add a Bob subcategory, another for Lisa, and so on for the entire family, all under the Medical category. The trouble with this is that you would need to create such subcategories for every category that could be assigned to a different family member. Pretty soon, you'd have about a zillion categories and subcategories. Instead, it's better to create a class for each family member and then assign that class to transactions as necessary.

Unlike categories, preset classes don't come with Quicken; you'll have to create and define your own. Like subcategories, subclasses are easy to create.

To create a class or subclass:

1. Choose Lists > Classes, or press ⌘K.
   The Classes window appears (**Figure 3.6**).

2. Click the New button.
   The Set Up Class window appears (**Figure 3.7**).

3. If you're creating a subclass, select the parent class, and then click the Add Subclass button.

4. Enter the name and (optionally) the description of the class, and then click the Create button.
   The name of the new class appears in the Classes window.

To edit or delete a class or subclass:

1. Select the category or subcategory in the Classes window.

2. Click the Edit button.
   The Edit Class window appears, which works in the same way as the Set Up Class window.

3. Make your changes, and then click the Change button.
   or
   To delete, follow step 1 above, and then click the Delete button. When Quicken asks you to confirm the deletion, click the Yes button.

Figure 3.6 Click the New button in the Classes window to create a new class.

Figure 3.7 Enter the name and description of the new class here.

✔ Tips

- Classes are a great way to differentiate personal and business expenses. For example, you can create a class called Business and assign it to categories that you also use for personal expenses. (For example, you can classify some meals as Dining/Business.)

- If you have many clients, you can use classes to track income expenses for each client separately. In the same way, you can create classes for projects or particular jobs.

- You can't change a class into a category or vice versa.

- If you rename a class, category, subclass, or subcategory, Quicken replaces the old name with the new one in all transactions that contained the old name.

- The items in the Categories & Transfers window and Classes window can be moved in the list by dragging them up or down. In this way, it's easy to demote a category to a subcategory or a class to a subclass, or to promote one to another.

USING CLASSES

USING THE
ACCOUNT REGISTERS

4

A *transaction* can be anything that changes the balance of an account. For a checking account, it could be writing a check, making a deposit, or withdrawing cash from the ATM. For a credit card account, it could be making a payment or a purchase. And for a stock portfolio account, transactions include buying shares and reinvesting dividends.

Every account in Quicken has an account register in which you enter transactions. Quicken's registers look and act much like paper checkbook registers, which makes them familiar and easy to use. One nice difference from paper, however, is that a Quicken register does the math for you and keeps a running balance automatically.

In this chapter, you'll learn how to enter transactions in the account registers, how to enter your paycheck into Quicken, how to use Quicken to keep track of your credit cards, and how to use Quicken's data entry aids to save you typing and time.

Entering Checking Account Transactions

Checks, deposits, and transfers are all transactions that need to be entered in your *account register*. An account register (**Figure 4.1**) contains all the information (in boxes called *fields*) you need about a transaction, including date, check number, payee, payment or deposit amount, category, memo field, and a check box to indicate whether the transaction has cleared your bank.

Checks that you intend to print from within Quicken can be entered either in the register or in the Write Checks window. (See Chapter 6 for more about printing checks.)

You enter information in a register by typing in a field and then pressing the Tab key to move to the next field.

To enter a check or a deposit:

1. Select your account from the Account buttons in the tool bar (**Figure 4.2**), or click the Registers button and choose an account from the pop-up menu (**Figure 4.3**). You can also pull down the Lists > Registers menu (**Figure 4.4**) and pick an account from there.

2. The account register opens with the Date field highlighted and the current date filled in. If you want to change the date, type in a new date, or click the calendar icon underneath the date (**Figure 4.5**), or use the date keyboard shortcuts shown in **Table 4.1.**

3. Press the Tab key to move to the Number field.

Figure 4.1 Enter transaction information in boxes called fields in the account register.

Figure 4.2 Clicking one of the Account buttons on the tool bar opens the account register.

Figure 4.3 Choose a checking account from the pop-up menu.

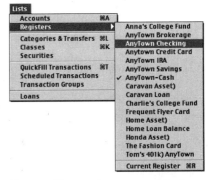

Figure 4.4 You can also open a register from the menu bar.

Figure 4.5 Click the calendar icon to change the date.

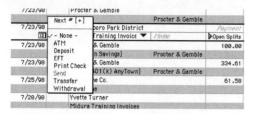

Figure 4.6 Choose a transaction type from the pop-up menu in the Number field.

Table 4.1

Keyboard shortcuts for the Date field	
SHORTCUT	WHAT IT DOES
+	Next day
–	Previous day
t	Today
m	Beginning of the current month
h	End of the current month
y	Beginning of the current year
r	End of the current year
[	Same date last month
]	Same date next month
{	Same date last year
}	Same date next year

Table 4.2

Keyboard shortcuts for the Number field	
SHORTCUT	WHAT IT DOES
+	Enters the next check number
–	Subtracts a check number
a	ATM, an ATM transaction
d	DEP, a deposit
e	EFT, Electronic Funds Transfer
p	PRINT, a check to be printed
s	SEND, an electronic payment to be sent
t	TRANS, a transfer to another Quicken account
x	XFR, a transfer to another Quicken account (old, but still works)
w	WITHD, a cash withdrawal

4. If you're writing a check, enter the next check number in the Number field. To have Quicken automatically enter the next number in your check sequence, press the ⊞ key. If you're entering another kind of transaction, choose that transaction type from the pop-up menu in the Number field (**Figure 4.6**).

See **Table 4.2** for the keyboard shortcuts you can use for transaction types.

5. Tab and enter the payee (for a check) or a description (for a deposit or transfer).

6. Tab across to the Payment or Deposit field and enter the amount.

7. Assign a category to the transaction by typing it into the Category field. The QuickFill feature fills in a category name from your list after you enter the first few letters. (See Chapter 5, and see the tips below, for more information about QuickFill.) You can also use the pop-up menu in the Category field to select the category.

8. If you want to add a class to the category, type a slash (/) at the end of the category name, and then type the class name (optional).

9. Enter a memo about the transaction (optional).

10. Click the Record button or press Enter. Quicken saves the transaction and adds it to the register.

(continued)

ENTERING CHECKING ACCOUNT TRANSACTIONS

✔ Tips

- To use the [Return] key instead of the [Tab] key to move from field to field, choose Edit > Preferences and then click the Register icon in the left side of the window. Click the check box next to "Pressing Return tabs to the next field."

- If you need to write a post-dated check, simply enter a future date in the Date field. At the bottom of the register, Quicken will display the "Balance Today" and a future balance showing the balance as of the date of the post-dated check.

- To quickly enter a date in the current month, type the day in the Date field and press the [Tab] key. Quicken automatically enters the current month and year.

- You can't type a value in the Balance column because Quicken does the math for you.

- To prevent QuickFill from filling in information on a particular entry, hold down the [Option] key as you tab to the next field.

- You can turn off QuickFill entirely from the Edit > Preferences menu.

- You can enter ATM withdrawals quickly by using QuickFill and starting your description with a number. For example, if you regularly withdraw $80, use the description *80 ATM*. The next time you record an ATM withdrawal, simply type *80* in to the Description field and Quicken will automatically fill in the rest of the information.

- In any field in which QuickFill works, you can use the up and down arrow keys to scroll alphabetically through the possible matches. For example, if you type "Ho" in the Description field, QuickFill might guess "Home Depot." Pressing the down arrow key would tell QuickFill to try the next possibility in the QuickFill list, "Home Savings." Pressing the up arrow key scrolls up alphabetically.

ENTERING CHECKING ACCOUNT TRANSACTIONS

Splitting Transactions

Many transactions need to be divided among multiple categories. This is called *splitting the transaction*. For example, you might write a single check at a service station that covers both gasoline and auto repairs. When you enter that transaction, you will enter a category name and amount for each part of the split. You can split checks that you write or payments that you receive.

To split a transaction:

1. In the register, enter the date, check number, payee, and the payment or deposit amount.

2. Click the Open Split button (it doesn't look like a button, but it really is), choose Edit > Split Transaction from the menu or press ⌘E. The split lines (where you enter additional categories and amounts) appear in the register (**Figure 4.7**).

3. Enter the category in the first Category field in the split, either by typing it in or by choosing it from the pop-up menu.

4. Type a memo in the first Memo field (optional).

5. Type the amount you want to allocate to the first category in the first Amount field.

   Quicken subtracts that amount from the total and puts the remainder in the next Amount field.

6. Enter the next category and amount on the next line. Repeat this until you have allocated the entire payment or deposit amount (**Figure 4.8**).

7. Click the Record button. The transaction is saved, properly allocated to multiple categories.

Figure 4.7 Use split lines to indicate separate payment categories in the register.

Figure 4.8 Enter category and amount information until you have allocated the entire payment or deposit amount.

✔ Tips

- If you want to split amounts but don't want to figure the total amount by adding yourself, Quicken adds up the total for you. For example, if you make one deposit that includes several checks from different categories, enter the amounts in all the split lines. As you add information, Quicken updates the total amount in the Deposit field.

- If you decide that you don't want to split the transaction after all, click the Clear Split button, which deletes all the information in the split lines.

- You can keep QuickFill from filling in splits by pressing Option Tab to exit the Payee field. Quicken clears all of the QuickFill information except for the payee name.

- You can add as many lines of categories as you need to a split transaction.

SPLITTING TRANSACTIONS

Entering Paychecks

You enter paychecks as split transactions, but with a bit of a difference: Because paychecks are subject to payroll deductions, you need to show the gross amount and the deductions in the split lines.

To enter a paycheck:

1. Open a checking account register.

2. Enter the date, press the [D] key to add *DEP* to the Number field, enter a description, and then enter the net amount of your paycheck in the Deposit field. The net is your salary minus all the deductions: in other words, the amount of the check.

3. Click the Split button, opening the split lines.

4. In the first Category field, enter *Salary*.

5. Enter a memo in the Memo field (optional).

6. Enter the gross amount of your salary in the first Amount field. The gross amount is the amount you're paid before deductions.

7. In the next Category field, enter the first category for your deductions. For example, you might want to use *Taxes:Federal* as the category.

8. In this and all subsequent split lines, enter your deductions as negative amounts so they will be subtracted from the gross (**Figure 4.9**). Keep adding lines until all your deductions are allocated.

9. Click the Record button.

✔ Tip

■ Most people's paychecks don't change very often. You can save a lot of repetitive data entry by selecting the transaction and choosing Edit > Memorize Transaction, or pressing ⌘M to memorize the amount.

Figure 4.9 Enter your deductions as negative amounts so they will be subtracted from the gross amount.

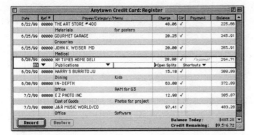

Figure 4.10 Enter information in the Charge and Payment fields in the credit card register.

Entering Credit Card Charges

Entering transactions in a credit card register is a lot like using a bank account register except that the headings "Charge" and "Payment" appear rather than "Payment" and "Deposit" (**Figure 4.10**). Another difference is that in a credit card register, you prefer a zero balance—something most people wouldn't want to see in their checking account.

To enter credit card charges:

1. Select your credit card account from the Account buttons in the tool bar, or click the Registers button and choose an account from the pop-up menu.

   The account register opens with the current date filled in and the Date field highlighted.

2. If you want to change the date, you can type in a new date, or click the calendar icon underneath the date, or use the date keyboard shortcuts shown in **Table 4.1**.

   Notice that instead of the Check number field, an optional Reference number field appears.

3. Enter the payee and the amount of the charge.

4. Enter the category.

5. Enter a memo about the charge (optional).

6. Click the Record button or press (Enter).

✔ Tips

■ You can dramatically reduce your data entry in credit card accounts by setting up the account for online banking, which lets you download all the transactions from the bank to the account register. See Chapter 11 for more information.

■ Don't forget to enter finance charges.

Transferring Money Between Accounts

Because you often need to transfer money between accounts, Quicken provides a way to perform this transaction. For example, when you write a check to make a payment to your credit card account, money flows out of the checking account and into the credit card account, decreasing the credit card's balance. Quicken makes it easy to update both accounts with one transaction so you don't have to enter the same transaction in both registers. To accomplish this, Quicken uses special categories called transfer categories, which refer to other Quicken accounts. You can view the transfer categories in your data file by choosing Lists > Categories & Transfers and scrolling to the bottom of the window (**Figure 4.11**). The transfer categories are the ones enclosed in the square brackets ([ ]).

In the first example below, you'll see how to use transfer categories to transfer money from your checking to your savings account. The next example shows you how to use the Transfer Money command to transfer money between accounts.

To transfer money from one account to another:

1. Select the account from which you want to move money from the Account buttons in the tool bar, or click the Registers button and choose it from the pop-up menu. You can also pull down the Lists > Registers menu and select an account from there.

    The account register opens with the Date field highlighted and the current date filled in.

Figure 4.11 You can view the transfer categories in your data file by scrolling to the bottom of the Categories & Transfers window.

Figure 4.12 Click the Record button and Quicken saves the transaction.

Figure 4.13 You can see a parallel transaction in the savings account register.

2. If you want to change the date, you can type in a new date, or click the calendar icon underneath the date, or use the date keyboard shortcuts shown in **Table 4.1.**

3. Press the ⟨Tab⟩ key and type *t* in the Number field. Quicken will enter *TRANS* to signify that this is a transfer.

4. Enter a description of the transfer in the Payee field.

5. Enter the amount in either the Payment or Deposit field, depending on whether you are moving money into or out of this account. (In this example, money is moving from this checking account to savings, so we enter the amount in the first Amount field. If the money were flowing from savings to checking, you would put the amount in the second field.)

6. In the Category field, press the left bracket (⟨[⟩) key, and then type the name of the account to which you want to transfer money.

   or

   Choose the savings account from the pop-up menu in the Category field. Your register should now look something like **Figure 4.12.**

7. Click the Record button.

   Quicken saves the transaction in the checking account register and creates a parallel transaction in the savings account register (**Figure 4.13**).

To use the Transfer Money command:

1. Choose Activities > Transfer Money.

   The Transfer Money Between Quicken Registers window appears (**Figure 4.14**).

2. Enter the date, a description in the Payee field (Transfer appears here by default), the amount you want to transfer, and a memo (optional).

3. Using the "From" pop-up menu, choose the source account for the transfer.

4. Using the "To" pop-up menu, choose the destination account for the transfer.

5. Click the Transfer button.

   Quicken creates entries in both the source and destination accounts.

Figure 4.14 Enter transaction information in the Transfer Money Between Quicken Registers window.

Figure 4.15 Click Yes to confirm the transaction deletion.

Changing Transactions

Unlike some other financial programs, Quicken allows you to make changes to transactions at any time. You can edit, delete, or void transactions whenever necessary.

To edit a transaction:

1. Open the account register that contains the transaction you want to edit.

2. Click on a transaction to select it.

3. In any field of the transaction, select the incorrect information and type over it to replace it.

4. Click the Record button.

To delete a transaction:

1. Open the account register that contains the transaction you want to delete.

2. Click on a transaction to select it.

3. Choose Edit > Delete Transaction, or press ⌘ D.
   Quicken will ask you to confirm the deletion (**Figure 4.15**).

4. Click the Yes button.
   Quicken deletes the transaction.

To void a transaction:

1. Open the account register that contains the transaction you want to void.

2. Click on a transaction to select it.

3. Choose Edit > Void Transaction. Quicken removes the amount in the Payment or Deposit field and places the word *VOID* at the beginning of the Payee field.

4. Click the Record button.

CHANGING TRANSACTIONS

To find a transaction:

1. Open the account register in which you want to find a transaction.

2. Choose Edit > Find/Replace > Find, or press ⌘F.
   The Find dialog box appears (**Figure 4.16**).

3. In the Find field, enter the text that you wish to search for. Make choices from the "Search" and "Match if" pop-up menus to narrow your search.

4. Click the Next button to find the next occurrence of your search text.

5. When you're done with your search, click the Close box in the Find window.

✔ Tips

- This feature is most useful when you're entering a transaction and wish to be reminded of the details of a previous transaction.

- When you're looking for multiple transactions, you're better off switching to the Reports section and running a QuickReport. See Chapter 12 for more information about reports.

Figure 4.16 Enter the text that you wish to search for in the Find field.

Figure 4.17 Enter the numbers you wish to calculate, pressing an operator key between each number.

Using Data Entry Helpers

Two other useful data entry tools you should know about are QuickMath and QuickEntry. QuickMath lets you make simple mathematical calculations right in the account register, and QuickEntry allows you to enter transactions without even opening Quicken.

QuickMath

QuickMath gives you a simple "paper tape" calculator right in the account register. If you want to make simple calculations while entering a transaction—for example adding up a bunch of checks while you're filling out the deposit transaction—QuickMath will make it easier.

To use QuickMath:

1. Begin entering a transaction in an account register.

2. For any field in which you can enter an amount, press an arithmetic operator key (+, –, *, /, or =) to pop up a "paper tape." You can enter numbers here as you would on an adding machine (**Figure 4.17**).

3. Enter the numbers you wish to calculate, pressing an operator key between each number. When you have entered all your numbers, click the Total button at the bottom of the paper tape. Quicken does the calculation and places the result in the amount field.

QuickEntry

If you enter transactions every day (and even if you don't), QuickEntry can reduce the time it takes. QuickEntry is a small application that opens quickly and lets you enter data into all of your bank, credit card, and cash account registers. You enter transactions into QuickEntry in exactly the same way you would into Quicken. QuickEntry data is stored in your Quicken data file and added to your Quicken registers the next time you open the Quicken program.

To use QuickEntry:

1. Choose QuickEntry from the Apple menu.

   The QuickEntry window appears (**Figure 4.18**).

2. Choose the account to which you want to enter data from the Account pop-up menu.

   After you make the change, the Ending Balance for that account is displayed in QuickEntry's lower right corner.

3. Enter transactions as you would in any Quicken register, clicking the Record button after each entry.

4. When you're done making entries, choose File > Quit.

5. The next time you open your Quicken data file, the QuickEntry Transactions window will appear (**Figure 4.19**), recapping the entries you made in QuickEntry. Click the OK button and Quicken adds the QuickEntry transactions to your registers and removes those entries from QuickEntry.

Figure 4.18 Choose QuickEntry from the Apple menu to open the QuickEntry window.

Figure 4.19 Click the OK button and Quicken will add the QuickEntry transactions to your registers.

ALL ABOUT QUICKFILL

5

If your financial situation is anything like mine, you find yourself repeating similar transactions over and over. For example, you probably make a rent or mortgage payment every month and deposit your paycheck biweekly or once a month. You probably also pay many of the same bills every month—to the phone company, to your electric utility, to your supermarket for groceries, whatever. You could simply type in all of that stuff again and again and again, but why bother? That's the kind of repetitive dog work for which computers were designed. You can let your computer remember and enter the boring stuff by using the QuickFill feature in Quicken.

QuickFill watches over your shoulder as you type information into an account register or onto a check. When the information you're typing matches a previous transaction, QuickFill enters the rest of the transaction for you. QuickFill can remember all or part of a transaction, so you can use it to remember and enter transactions whose amounts stay the same every month (such as your rent or mortgage payment) or transactions that can change each month (like the electric bill).

In this chapter, you'll learn how to use QuickFill to make entering transactions easier and to memorize, edit, enter, and delete QuickFill transactions.

How QuickFill Works

Let's face it—there's nothing especially fun or glamorous about entering your transactions into an account register. In fact, it can be downright dull. QuickFill is an important tool that helps you get information into Quicken fast and with less boredom.

Every time you enter a transaction in your account register or on a check, Quicken adds the information to the QuickFill Transaction list. Then, when you create a new entry, Quicken compares the information in the QuickFill list to what you're typing. As soon as it finds a match, QuickFill fills in the rest of the transaction for you. If QuickFill's guess is correct, all you'll probably need to do is change the amount of that particular check. If QuickFill guesses wrong, you keep typing and your entry will replace QuickFill's guess.

You can also manually add transactions to QuickFill's list by selecting a transaction and manually "memorizing" it. You can view, use, edit, or delete QuickFill transactions via the QuickFill Transactions window (**Figure 5.1**).

✔ Tips

- If you hold down the Option key when you tab from the Payee field to the Amount field, Quicken removes its QuickFill guesses from the Amount and Category fields.

- Keep in mind that Quicken won't add information to the QuickFill list from the account registers in the Investing section.

- You can turn QuickFill on or off, and you can turn off the automatic updating of the QuickFill list. To do so, choose Edit > Preferences to open the Preferences window. Click the Register icon. Then click on or off the check boxes next to "Use QuickFill to fill in transactions" and "Add new transactions to the QuickFill list" (**Figure 5.2**).

Figure 5.1 The QuickFill Transactions list helps you save a tremendous amount of time and keystrokes.

Figure 5.2 You can turn QuickFill on or off in the Register Preferences window.

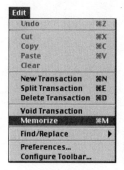

Figure 5.3 Quicken indicates locked transactions by adding a black dot to the left of the transaction in the QuickFill list.

Figure 5.4 Quicken indicates which transaction is selected in a register by adding a border around it.

Figure 5.5 Choose Memorize from the Edit menu, or press ⌘M.

Memorizing Transactions

Usually you won't need to do anything to memorize a transaction and add it to the QuickFill Transactions list. Quicken will do it for you automatically. See for yourself: You have already entered some data into Quicken, so open the QuickFill Transactions list by choosing Lists > QuickFill Transactions to see the automatically memorized transactions.

Sometimes, however, you'll want to *manually* memorize a transaction, usually because you want to *lock* or *unlock* it. The black dots that appear at the left of the transactions in **Figure 5.3** indicate locked transactions. You can unlock transactions so that QuickFill will memorize any changes, or you can lock them so that the QuickFill entry will not update should you make any changes to the register entry.

Unlocked transactions are typically used for transactions that are written to the same payee but with different details. For example, you might often write checks to Safeway, but the amount and even the category might vary with every check.

Locked QuickFill transactions are useful for checks written to the same payee for which the details rarely change, such as a car payment. You can still change the amount in the register or on the check, but that won't affect the memorized amount stored in a locked QuickFill transaction.

To manually memorize a QuickFill transaction:

1. In your account register, select a transaction by clicking it. Quicken adds a border around the transaction you selected (**Figure 5.4**).

2. Choose Edit > Memorize (**Figure 5.5**), or press ⌘M.

Using QuickFill Transactions

QuickFill usually works unobtrusively, automatically popping in information as you enter transactions in account registers or on checks. But you can also use the QuickFill Transactions list manually to help you add transactions by keeping the QuickFill Transactions list open while entering data.

Why would you want to do this? Here's one example. I use three telephone lines in my house, one personal, the other two business related, so I track expenditures on all three separately. Naturally, the lines are all maintained by the same phone company, so the payee is the same. If I used QuickFill in the usual fashion, I couldn't track which QuickFill transactions cover the personal line and which ones cover the business lines. So I open the QuickFill Transactions window, where each transaction includes a Memo field indicating the type of phone line to which the transaction applies.

To use the QuickFill Transactions list to help enter transactions:

1. With your account register open, choose Lists > QuickFill Transactions, or press ⌘T. The QuickFill Transactions window opens (**Figure 5.6**).

2. Scroll through the QuickFill Transactions list until you find the transaction that you want to use.

3. Click on the transaction to highlight it.

4. Click the Use button to transfer the contents of the transaction to the open account register. Or, drag a transaction from the QuickFill Transactions window and drop it on the account register. Or, even simpler, double-click the transaction to enter it in the account register.

Figure 5.6 You can enter QuickFill transactions manually.

Figure 5.7 You can edit a transaction in the Edit QuickFill Transaction window.

Editing QuickFill Transactions

You can change any part of a QuickFill transaction, although you won't usually need to. Most often, you'll clear the amount of a transaction and then lock the transaction so that in future transactions with the same payee, you'll simply fill in the amount of the check.

To edit a QuickFill transaction:

1. Open the QuickFill Transactions window.

2. Click once on the transaction that you want to edit to select it.

3. Click the Edit button at the bottom of the QuickFill Transaction window.
   The Edit QuickFill Transaction window appears (**Figure 5.7**).

4. Make any needed changes in the Payee or Description, Payment, Category/Class, Memo, or Amount fields. Notice that you can use split transactions here (see Chapter 4).

5. To replace the transaction with your changes, click the Replace button. Or, to create a new QuickFill transaction with the edited information, click the Add button. Or, to back out of the window without saving changes, click the Cancel button.

To lock or unlock a QuickFill transaction:

1. Follow steps 1 through 4 above.

2. To lock a transaction, click the "Locked" check box in the Edit QuickFill Transaction window. To unlock the transaction, clear the "Locked" check box.

3. The QuickFill Transactions list indicates locked transactions by adding a black dot next to them (refer to **Figure 5.3**).

Deleting QuickFill Transactions

You might choose to get rid of a QuickFill transaction because it lists a payee that you dealt with only once, or to eliminate duplicate entries.

To delete a QuickFill transaction:

1. In the QuickFill Transactions window, click once on the transaction that you want to eliminate.

   Quicken highlights the memorized transaction.

2. Click the Delete button at the bottom of the QuickFill Transactions window.

3. Click Yes when Quicken asks you to confirm the deletion.

✔ Tips

- If you leave a QuickFill transaction unlocked, Quicken replaces the amount of the check in the transaction every time you use the QuickFill entry. The next time you use that QuickFill entry, you'll see the amount of the last check you wrote to that payee. This makes it easy to tell if your spending with that payee has changed drastically. If it has, you have a chance to either rethink your spending pattern or check for an error in the current month's bill. I once found a $75 error in a utility bill in this fashion.

- If a loan transaction is listed in your QuickFill Transactions list, you won't be able to edit it from the QuickFill Transactions window. You'll need to go to the Loans window (choose Lists > Loans). For more about changing loan information, see Chapter 14.

WRITING AND PRINTING CHECKS

Just to avoid any possible confusion, this chapter is about writing checks that you intend to print from Quicken, on preprinted check forms. Checks that you write by hand should be entered into Quicken in your checking account register, as shown in Chapter 4.

If you don't already use Quicken to print your checks on preprinted check forms, you should definitely reconsider. When I was researching this book, I discovered that a surprising number of people don't use the program's printing abilities. If you're one of those folks, you're missing out on a lot of convenience. Consider: when you write checks by hand in your regular checkbook, you first fill out the check. Then you'll have to type all the same information into Quicken's check register. That's a lot of double work.

Using Quicken to print your checks can also help you avoid errors. Before I started printing checks, I'd discover (usually after chasing numbers for a good half hour when balancing my checkbook) that I had typed an incorrect amount for a handwritten check into the Quicken register. But when you write a check in Quicken in the first place, there's no chance of a pesky typo wasting your time later, because Quicken automatically enters each check amount into its register. It makes checkbook balancing much faster.

To write a check:

1. Open the Write Checks window by choosing Activities > Write Checks, by pressing ⌘J, or by clicking the Checks button on the task bar (**Figure 6.1**). The Write Checks window for your main checking account appears (**Figure 6.2**).

2. In the Write Checks window, today's date is entered for you and highlighted. If you want to change the date, type in a new date.

   or

   Click the Calendar button in the Write Checks window and a small calendar will pop up (**Figure 6.3**). Click on the new date in the small calendar window to add that date to the check.

3. Type in the name of the payee. As you type, QuickFill will anticipate and fill in the payee's name if what you're typing is similar to a name that appears on a previously written check. (See Chapter 5 for more about QuickFill.)

4. QuickFill puts in the same amount that appeared in the last transaction with the payee unless the QuickFill entry is locked; this is handy for checks that you write each month for the same amount. Press the Tab key to move on if the amount is correct. If it's not correct, fill in the amount of the check.

   On the next line, Quicken turns the amount you entered into its text form. (For $42.76, for example, Quicken enters Forty-two and 76/100.)

5. Enter the name and address of the payee in the Address field (optional). To copy and paste the payee's name into the first line of the Address field, press the single quotation mark (') key.

Figure 6.1 Click the Checks button in the task bar to open the Write Checks window.

Figure 6.2 The Write Checks window looks like a real check, and you fill it out in much the same way that you fill out a regular check.

Figure 6.3 You can choose a date for the check from the calendar pop-up window.

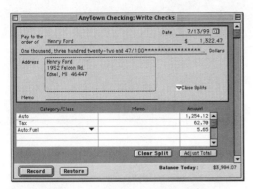

Figure 6.4 Your completed check should look something like this.

Figure 6.5 Use the Register section of Quicken's Preferences window to turn on a note field on checks.

Figure 6.6 Type your account number on a check in the note line.

6. Fill in the Memo field to record a memo about this check (optional).

7. If QuickFill entered the appropriate payee in step 3, it probably filled in the Category field correctly as well, and you can move on to the next step. Otherwise, type in the appropriate category or use the Category pop-up menu to select one. You can use split transactions if you need to.

8. Click the Record button or press the [Enter] key. The completed check should look similar to that shown in **Figure 6.4**.

✔ Tips

■ The Write Checks window is usually the one for your main checking account (you can tell which account you're using because the name of the account shows up in the title bar of the Write Checks window), but you can force it to appear for other accounts from which you can write checks. Just open the account's register for that account before you open the Write Checks window.

■ If you mail your printed checks in a windowed mailing envelope, the Memo line may be visible through the window. Adding confidential account numbers to the Memo line would be unsuitable. You can use another space to add these numbers. Choose Edit > Preferences, click the Register icon, and click "Show additional note on checks" (**Figure 6.5**). A note line will appear on the check (**Figure 6.6**). You can fill in this note line only from the Write Checks window; the account register doesn't show it. This note line also won't appear in the envelope window.

■ To memorize transactions in the Write Checks window as well as in the account register, choose Edit > Memorize or press ⌘ M.

WRITING CHECKS

55

To edit a check:

1. Use the vertical scroll bar in the Write Checks window to scroll through checks you've written in the current session.

2. Find the check and edit the information.

3. Click the Record button or press the [Enter] key to save your work.

✔ Tip

■ If you prefer, you can edit the check by making changes in the account register. (See Chapter 4 for how to use the account register.) After you print a check, it disappears from the Write Checks window and is entered in the account register. Note that the check is accessible only from the account register after it has been printed.

To delete a check:

1. Scroll in the Write Checks window until you find the check you want to delete.

2. Choose Edit > Delete Transaction, or press [⌘][D]. Quicken will pop up a dialog box asking you if you're sure you want to delete this check.

3. Click the Yes button to confirm the deletion.

✔ Tips

■ You can neither delete a check nor edit check information from the Write Checks window after the check has been printed. If you need to change or delete check information after you have printed a check, you can access the information from the account register. See Chapter 4 for more information.

■ Looking to void a check? You have to do that in the account register. See "Voiding Transactions" in Chapter 4 for more information.

Ordering Checks

You can buy checks preprinted with your name, address, bank name and account number, check numbers, and any other information required by your bank. These checks are designed for use in laser printers and ink jet printers (you can also order continuous checks for dot-matrix printers), and they generally come in one of three styles:

- ◆ Standard Checks are sized for use in a business-size envelope and come three to a page (**Figure 6.7**).

- ◆ Voucher Checks are good for payroll and accounts payable use; you get one check per page, with two check stubs that you can keep or send out with the check as needed (**Figure 6.8**).

- ◆ Wallet Checks are smaller than standard checks (so that they can, not surprisingly, fit into your wallet) and include a stub for recording check information when writing a check by hand (**Figure 6.9**).

After you decide which style makes the most sense for you, have your current checkbook ready (you'll need it for the bank information and your account number) and order your checks. But where to get computer checks? One place is from Intuit itself, although they tend to charge more than some other companies. Many other business supply companies can provide checks and save you some money. See **Table 6.1** for some suggestions.

Figure 6.7 Standard checks are the ones used by most people, because they're the most convenient.

Figure 6.8 Voucher checks are good if you need a paper trail of check stubs. But for most of us, the less paper, the better.

Figure 6.9 Wallet-style checks make sense if you want to carry your computer checks with you.

Table 6.1

Sources for Computer Checks

COMPANY	PHONE NUMBER	URL
Intuit	800-787-6748	www.intuitmarketplace.com
NEBS	800-225-6380	www.nebs.com
Checks for Less	800-325-5568	www.checksforless.com
PC Checks	800-322-5317	www.pcchecks.com
Sensible Solutions	888-852-4325	www.sensible-solutions.com

Getting Ready to Print

After you have entered your checks for print-ing in the Write Checks window or in the account register, you're almost ready to print. But first you must set up Quicken to use your checks.

To set up Quicken to print:

1. From the Apple menu, select Chooser.

2. In the Chooser window (**Figure 6.10**), select the printer you want to use, and then close the window.

3. In Quicken, choose Edit > Preferences.

4. Click the Print Checks icon from the scrolling panel on the left (**Figure 6.11**).

5. Each bank account can have its own Print Checks settings. From the Account pop-up menu, choose the account to which you want these set-tings to apply.

6. Choose the font and font size you want printed on your checks.

7. Pick a style (standard, voucher, or wal-let) from the Check Style pop-up menu.

8. Depending on how your particular printer feeds paper, choose one of the four alignments when printing one or two checks.

9. Unless you have a continuous-feed printer, leave the Sheet feeder check box checked.

10. If you're using voucher checks, check the "Print categories on voucher checks" check box.

11. Click the OK button to save your set-tings for this checking account.

Figure 6.10 Select which printer you want to use from the Chooser window. For most printers, Quicken's default settings will do just fine.

Figure 6.11 In the Print Checks Preferences window, you can create different check printing settings for each account. Clicking the CheckArt button allows you to print an image, such as a logo, on your checks.

Figure 6.12 Clicking the Print Checks button on the task bar is your entrée to check-printing bliss.

Figure 6.13 The Print Checks window tells you how many checks are set to print.

Figure 6.14 If you want to print particular checks, use the Select Checks to Print dialog box.

Printing Checks

Now that you've set up Quicken's printing functions, it's finally time to print. Note that most of the setup needs to be done only once; you'll just be printing merrily away.

To print checks:

1. Make sure the checks are in your printer tray and positioned correctly for printing. You might want to run a test on some plain paper before you print on real checks for the first time.

2. Verify that your printer is turned on and that it is online.

3. Open the account from which you want to print checks.

4. Choose File > Print Checks, or press ⌘P, or click the Print Checks button from the task bar (**Figure 6.12**). The Print Checks window appears (**Figure 6.13**), telling you how many checks are ready to print.

5. The starting check number should match the first number of the checks that you put in the printer. If it doesn't match, change it. (In the future, Quicken will remember the number of the last check that you printed and automatically add the next number in this space.)

6. Add a date in the "Checks dated through" box to print all checks written up to this date. You'll probably use this option most often.

   or

   Click the Selected Checks radio button to open the Select Checks to Print dialog box (**Figure 6.14**). In the Print column, put a checkmark next to the checks that you want to print, and then click OK.

(continued)

PRINTING CHECKS

7. In the Print Checks window, click Print to open the printer dialog box.

8. Click the Print button in the printer dialog box to start printing checks.

9. After the checks have been printed, Quicken will ask you whether all the checks printed correctly (**Figure 6.15**). If they did, click Yes and Quicken will enter the check numbers into the account register.

If any of the checks did not print correctly (usually because of a printer problem), click No and Quicken will ask you to type in the number of the first incorrectly printed check. Fix the printer problem and start again at step 4 above to print the remaining checks.

Figure 6.15 Quicken needs reassurance that your checks printed correctly. Soothe it by clicking the Yes button.

✔ Tips

■ To stop printing in the middle of a print job, press ⌘⌐ (period).

■ You can reprint a check at any time (if a payee loses a check, for example). Just replace the check number in your register with the word PRINT, and click the Record button. Then print the check normally.

■ Quicken's User Manual includes a chart showing Mac printers and how to position checks in their printer trays for correct printing.

Writing Checks by Hand

When you're away from home, you can write checks with the checkbook that your bank provided when you opened your account, or you can use your preprinted computer checks and fill them out by hand. I like to use my regular bank checkbook and enter the information into Quicken when I return home. I differentiate between the checks that Quicken prints and ones I handwrite by using two widely different sets of check numbers for each kind of check. For example, I started my computer checks at 1000 and my handwritten checks start in the 4000 range. Quicken has no problem dealing with different sets of check numbers.

USING THE CALENDAR

When a bill gets paid is often as important as the amount of the payment. Because many of your financial transactions are time-sensitive, Quicken gives you a tool that lets you see your transactions over time: the Financial Calendar. With the Calendar, you can schedule future transactions and set up recurring transactions that need be paid on a regular schedule, such as mortgage payments or utility bills. Scheduled transactions can be entered automatically, saving you the drudgery of data entry. The Calendar can also remind you of upcoming payments and give you a quick visual overview of how you spend your money each month.

Two other Quicken features work with the Financial Calendar: the Scheduled Transactions list and Billminder. Scheduled transactions are memorized transactions (see Chapter 5) that get entered automatically when they're due. Billminder pops up when you start your computer and reminds you of scheduled transactions.

Working with the Calendar

To display the calendar, choose Activities > Calendar, or click the Calendar button in the task bar (**Figure 7.1**). The Financial Calendar will appear (**Figure 7.2**). The current day is automatically highlighted and each financial transaction you've made in the current month is listed in black text on its respective date. Scheduled transactions that have not yet been paid are listed in blue text.

The controls at the top of the Financial Calendar let you change the month or year that is displayed. Controls at the bottom of the calendar let you view transactions for your accounts and enter new transactions.

To add a new transaction:

1. In the Calendar, select the date on which you wish to schedule a transaction.

2. At the bottom of the Calendar window, click the New Transaction button. The Enter Transaction window appears (**Figure 7.3**). If you choose a future date, the same screen appears, this time labeled Schedule Future Transaction.

Figure 7.1 Click the Calendar button to display, well, the calendar.

Figure 7.2 If you like, you can do all your data entry in the Financial Calendar.

Figure 7.3 The Enter Transaction screen's default mode acts like an account register.

Figure 7.4 If you would rather pay your bills online, you can do so in the Enter Transaction window's online payment mode.

Figure 7.5 If you prefer printing checks, you can use write checks mode.

3. Using the buttons in the upper right corner of the Enter Transactions window, choose the mode in which you want to enter the transaction.

   By default, the Enter Transaction screen is set to account register mode, in which you can enter a transaction just as you enter a transaction into an account register. If you plan to create transactions that will be sent via online bill payment and have already enabled online bill payment (see Chapter 9), you can switch to that mode, as shown in **Figure 7.4**. Or you can enter calendar transactions in the familiar write checks mode, as shown in **Figure 7.5**.

4. Click on the down arrow in the Account area to see the Account pop-up menu. Choose the account against which you'll apply the transaction.

5. By default, the current date appears in the Date field. You can leave this date as is or change it to another date.

6. In account register mode, with the cursor in the Number field, press the plus key (+) on your keyboard to enter the next check number. If you plan to print the check, you could also type PRINT in the Number field.

   (continued)

WORKING WITH THE CALENDAR

7. Enter the payee's name. As you're typing, QuickFill looks at names it has learned. If it finds a match, it adds the name. If this name is incorrect, you can simply change it.

8. In the Payment field, enter the amount if QuickFill hasn't already.

9. Type in the category or click the down arrow in the Category area to select the category of the transaction.

10. Enter a memo about the transaction (optional).

11. If necessary, split the transaction. See Chapter 4 for more about splitting transactions.

12. If this is a one-time transaction, leave Frequency set to "Only once." If this will be a recurring transaction, select how often it will recur from the Frequency pop-up menu (**Figure 7.6**).

13. In the Duration area, select either the "Unlimited" or the "Stop after [blank] transactions" radio button and fill in the blank.

14. In the Future transactions pop-up menu, choose either "Remind me about" or "Automatically enter." Whichever you choose, to enter the information in advance of the selected date, fill in the "Days in Advance" field with a number.

15. Click Record to save the transaction.

```
Only once
Weekly
Every two weeks
Twice a month
Every four weeks
✓ Monthly
Last day of month
Every two months
Quarterly
Twice a year
Annually
```

Figure 7.6 The Frequency pop-up menu allows you to select how often a transaction will recur.

Figure 7.7 Double-click on a day in the Calendar window to open the Transactions window that lists all transactions scheduled for or that occurred on that day.

Figure 7.8 You can view upcoming transactions in the Scheduled Transactions window.

To edit a transaction:

1. In the Financial Calendar, double-click on the day that contains the transaction that you want to edit. The Transaction window for that day appears, as shown in **Figure 7.7**.

2. Double-click on the transaction that you want to edit. The Edit Transaction window, which looks and acts exactly like the Enter Transaction window, appears.

3. Make any changes you want, and then click the Record button.

To view scheduled transactions:

1. Choose Lists > Scheduled Transactions. A window appears showing you your upcoming transactions (**Figure 7.8**). The window shows recurring transactions with their frequency, so rather than listing every future instance of a transaction that happens twice a month, it only lists the transaction's next due date and "Twice a month" in the Frequency column.

2. You can create a new scheduled transaction or edit or delete existing transactions using the buttons at the bottom of the Scheduled Transactions window.

WORKING WITH THE CALENDAR

65

To delete a transaction:

1. In the Financial Calendar, double-click on the day that contains a transaction that you want to delete. The Transaction window for that day appears (see **Figure 7.7**).

2. Click the transaction to select it.

3. Click the Delete button in the Transactions window.

4. Quicken will ask you to confirm the deletion. Click the Yes button to delete the transaction.

5. Close the Transactions window.

✔ Tip

■ Remember that entering a transaction in the Calendar also enters it in an account register.

WORKING WITH THE CALENDAR

Figure 7.9 The Transactions Group window lets you view old groups or add new ones.

Figure 7.10 You can set up a transaction group in the Set Up Group window.

Transaction Groups

It's often more convenient to pay your bills in batches. For example, I have three telephone lines at my house, so I receive three different bills. Because I prefer to pay all three bills at the same time, I've created a transaction group in the Calendar that automatically enters three separate transactions simultaneously.

To create a transaction group:

1. Choose Lists > Transaction Groups. The Transaction Groups window appears, as shown in **Figure 7.9**.

2. Click the New button. The Set Up Group window appears, as shown in **Figure 7.10**.

3. In the field next to Group Name, type in a name for the transaction group.

4. From the pop-up menu next to Destination, choose the account from which the payments will be made.

5. In the Reminder Settings section, set the frequency for which the group transaction should recur, and then enter the next date for the group transaction. If you want the transactions entered automatically, mark that box.

6. Select the transactions that you want to include in the group. A check mark appears next to each selected transaction. If you make a mistake and need to deselect a transaction, click it again to remove the check mark.

7. Click the Create button.

To use a transaction group:

1. In the Transaction Group window, select a transaction group.

2. Click the Use button. The Recall Transaction Group dialog box appears (**Figure 7.11**).

3. Check that the settings in the dialog box are correct, and then click the OK button. Quicken will make the appropriate entries in the account register(s) and then open those registers for your inspection. If necessary, edit the transactions in the registers in the usual fashion.

Figure 7.11 The Recall Transaction Group dialog lets you add multiple entries in the account register in one step.

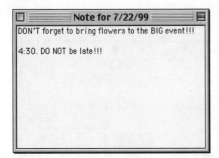

Figure 7.12 You can include any text that you want in the Calendar's note window.

Figure 7.13 Double-click the note icon to recall your note.

Adding Calendar Notes

In addition to showing transactions, the Calendar can also contain notes, kind of like yellow sticky notes, that contain virtually any information—from personal notes to to-do lists to additional notes on the financial transactions for that day.

To create a calendar note:

1. In the Calendar window, select a date to which you wish to add a note.

2. At the bottom of the Calendar window, click the Add Note button. The note window for that date appears.

3. Enter the text for the note (**Figure 7.12**).

4. Close the window to save the note.

5. Quicken adds a small note icon to the day in which you created the note (**Figure 7.13**). To read the note in the future, double-click the note icon.

Using Billminder

Billminder is a feature that you can set to alert you of scheduled transactions as soon as you start up your Mac. (Don't worry, you can turn it off if you want.) Quicken doesn't have to be running for Billminder to do its job. Once Billminder pops up (**Figure 7.14**), you can either run Quicken and deal with the reminders, or you can skip the reminders until the next time you start up the application.

To turn Billminder on:

1. Choose Edit > Preferences to open the Preferences dialog. Scroll down to the Billminder section (**Figure 7.15**).

2. Check either or both of the boxes in the Quicken will remind you area.

3. Set the days in advance field to whatever lead time you'd like. Click OK.

Figure 7.14 Billminder reminds you of pending–and overdue–transactions.

Figure 7.15 You can control the way Billminder works from the Preferences panel.

Using Quicken Insights

Quicken offers you a lot of control over your finances, and a virtual avalanche of supporting data that you can use to assess where you are in terms of reaching your financial goals. But this wealth of information, while useful, can also be overwhelming. It can take a long time to plow through several reports and registers to get the big picture of your investments, assets, and liabilities.

Quicken 2000's new Insights feature organizes all of your financial information onto one page. From this home page, you can get the big financial picture and evaluate how you are doing in any personal finance area without having to rummage through different reports. The Insights page includes tables, graphs, and hypertext links called Actions that let you perform a whole range of Quicken tasks.

In this chapter, you'll learn how to use and customize Quicken's Insights page to get the information that you need.

Using the Insights Page

The Insights page is kind of a one-stop-shopping presentation of your whole Quicken file. There are up to 12 areas in the window, ranging from a summary of your accounts to graphs of your Net Worth and your Income and Expenses (**Figure 8.1**). Insights can be set up to present as much or as little information as you want in a variety of different forms.

Each of the areas on the page is presented as a main display—either a list or a graph—and some Observations and Actions that allow you to do something with the information in front of you.

On the Insights page, you can use the various Actions options to customize the individual items, editing lists, changing date ranges, and so on.

To customize the Insights page:

1. Open Insights by choosing Activities > Insights or by clicking the Insights button on the tool bar (**Figure 8.2**).

2. In the upper right corner of the window, click the Customize button.

3. In the Customize Insights window (**Figure 8.3**), you can move items from the Available list to the Selected list and arrange the latter on the page with the Move Up and Move Down buttons.

4. When you're satisfied, click Done.

Figure 8.1 Quicken Insights presents huge amount of information in a compact form.

Figure 8.2 The Insights button on the tool bar takes you directly to the Insights page.

Figure 8.3 You can move items on or off the page from the Customize Insights dialog box.

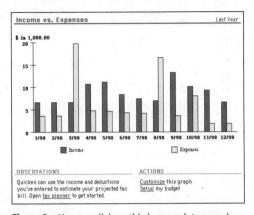

Figure 8.4 You can click on this bar graph to reveal more information, and the links below it can be useful as well.

Adding to Your Insights Page

From the Customize Insights window, you can choose any of the following for your own personal Insights. Putting these on the page gives you immediate access to them and makes it much easier for you to move among your various accounts.

◆ **Accounts** presents a list of all your Quicken accounts with their current balances, bank charges, and interest earned. It includes Actions to create new accounts, reconcile your accounts, get online transactions, and open your Financial Calendar.

◆ **Budgets** gives you a rundown on how well you are keeping to the budget you set up and helps you analyze your spending and even go online to learn how to reduce your debt.

◆ **Credit Card Analysis** shows your current charges, credit limits, and balances.

◆ **Expenses** shows a pie chart of your expenses by category and a detailed breakdown of your expenditures at the touch of a button.

◆ **Income vs. Expenses** (**Figure 8.4**) is a bar graph that compares these two key measures of financial well-being on a monthly (or other period) basis. It also links you to the budget setup window and the tax planner.

◆ **Income** tracks your various categories of income and compares them to the same period last year. It links to the Investment Returns area and to a calculation of your net worth.

(continued)

◆ **Investment Accounts** gives a capsule view of your money invested and links to your portfolio and to the online quote feature of Quicken.

◆ **Investment Returns** analyzes the performance of your investments.

◆ The **Loan Summary** section charts the balances and interest rates as well as the principle paid and the payments remaining on each of your loan accounts. It includes links to the Scheduled Transactions window to make payments and to the Web, where you can shop for mortgage rates.

◆ The **Net Worth Graph** area (**Figure 8.5**) graphs the change in your financial picture over time with the option of creating various detailed reports.

◆ **Scheduled Transactions** presents the information from the window of the same name in the main body of the Quicken program and provides a direct link to the Financial Calendar. Sometimes it gives you a gentle reminder that "you have scheduled transactions that need to be entered in the register."

◆ The **Watch List** (**Figure 8.6**) is a group of stocks and funds you have chosen to track online. Insights provides access to an extensive range of analytic tools and online research on the Quicken Web site.

Figure 8.5 The Net Worth graph contains a lot of useful information.

Figure 8.6 The Watch List allows you to quickly download current prices and news items for a preset list of securities.

Figure 8.7 You can customize individual displays from the dialog boxes that open from the main window.

Figure 8.8 The pie chart shows how your expenses are distributed over a number of categories.

Figure 8.9 The magnifying glass shows the dollar figure represented by the pie slice.

Diving Beneath the Surface

The amount of information you can access through the Insights page is not immediately obvious, but the mouse is a remarkably powerful tool here.

Clicking on an underlined link in the Actions area triggers that function; in this way, Insights acts like a Web page, because clicking a link makes something happen. If the display area contains a graph, holding the mouse cursor over a graph segment (you don't need to click on it) shows you the dollar amount of that segment, and double-clicking it opens a more detailed graph of the underlying data.

The following is an example of using the Insights window, using the Expenses pie chart as a starting point.

1. You can customize the chart by clicking on the Customize this Graph link at the bottom of the window and making your choices in the Customize Expense Comparison Graph window (**Figure 8.7**).

2. In the first view (**Figure 8.8**), last year's expenses have been divided into 11 categories, including that always useful "Other."

3. Moving the cursor over one of the segments (in this case, Taxes, **Figure 8.9**) turns it into a magnifying glass. Hold down the mouse button and up pops the dollar figure for the segment.

(continued)

4. Double-clicking produces a bar graph of the month-to-month expenditures for that category (**Figure 8.10**).

5. Again, the magnifying glass shows the dollar value of any individual month (**Figure 8.11**).

6. Double-clicking brings up a tax detail report for the month (**Figure 8.12**).

7. Double-clicking on a line of that report brings us all the way back to the register in which the item is entered (**Figure 8.13**).

Figure 8.10 Double-clicking on the pie chart opens a bar chart of one segment.

Figure 8.11 The magnifying glass shows the dollar value of each bar when the mouse button is held down.

Figure 8.12 A double-click opens a report page for the month.

Figure 8.13 Double-clicking on a line item takes you all the way back to the register entry.

DIVING BENEATH THE SURFACE

Figure 8.14 The Quicken Quotes server—and detailed security quotes—are just a click away.

Figure 8.15 You can find out more about an individual stock by clicking on the Research link below the Watch List or by clicking on the name of one of the stocks on your list.

Figure 8.16 The Quicken.com quote page is a treasure trove of investment information.

Figure 8.17 The Mortgage page has links to all kinds of tools, services, and assorted links.

On to the Internet

From other areas on the Insights page, you can jump to the Internet for more information and updates. Here are a few examples:

◆ Several of the investment related areas link directly to the Quicken Quotes server (**Figure 8.14**), to download current prices for your Watch List, or through the Research Security dialog box (**Figure 8.15**) to Quicken.com's investment page on the Internet (**Figure 8.16**). For more about using Quicken and the Web, see Chapter 19.

◆ The Net Worth and Loan Summary areas both have links to Quicken's mortgage page (**Figure 8.17**), which has a wealth of information and links to participating lenders.

◆ Budgets links to an online Debt Reduction Planner on Quicken.com's site (**Figure 8.18**) on the off-chance that your budget is not quite what it ought to be.

Figure 8.18 The Debt Reduction Planner is another example of the planning tools you can access on the Quicken Web site.

ON TO THE INTERNET

BALANCING
YOUR ACCOUNTS

9

Balancing your checkbook is one of Those Chores—things that everyone knows you need to do, that everyone claims to do regularly, but that surprisingly few people actually accomplish. And who can blame them? Balancing your checkbook by hand is a pain, especially if you have slacked off for a few months and need to catch up.

Tracking your checking account and balancing your checkbook is the number one reason why people buy Quicken to do it for them. Quicken does a great job of reconciling accounts, and it makes a chore that took an hour by hand easy to do in just a few minutes.

Quicken isn't limited to just reconciling your checkbook, however. You can balance your savings, money market, or credit card accounts, too. In addition to balancing accounts, you can update balances in cash, asset, or liability accounts to reflect transfers of funds, payments made, or interest received.

In this chapter, you'll learn how to reconcile accounts, update account balances, and resolve any differences between the bank's records and your own.

Balancing Accounts

You'll use the same procedure to balance a checking account, savings account, or money market account. First you enter your bank statement balance, and then you match transactions on your bank statement with transactions in your Quicken account register.

Balancing a credit card account works in almost the same way—except that if a balance is due on the credit card, Quicken will ask whether you want to make a payment at the end of the reconciliation process.

Before you begin, you should make sure that you have entered all transactions that occurred between the date of your last statement and the date of your current statement.

If you need to reconcile for more than one month, you first need to reconcile your account with the bank statements for each of the prior months before you try to reconcile the current month's statement.

To balance a checking, savings, or money market account:

1. Open the register for the account you want to balance by clicking its button (**Figure 9.1**) on the tool bar or by choosing Lists > Registers and selecting it on the list (**Figure 9.2**).

2. Click the Reconcile button in the tool bar (**Figure 9.3**) or choose Activities > Reconcile.

   The Reconcile Startup window appears (**Figure 9.4**).

3. Check to make sure that the beginning balance on your bank statement matches the amount in the Beginning Balance box in the Reconcile Startup window. If the amounts don't match, you'll need to click the Cancel button and fix the problem.

Figure 9.1 Click the account button on the tool bar to open the register.

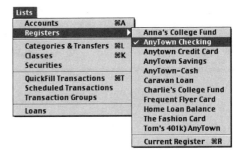

Figure 9.2 Select the account you wish to reconcile.

Figure 9.3 Click the Reconcile button to open the Reconcile Startup window.

Figure 9.4 Check to make sure that the beginning balance on your bank statement matches the amount in the Beginning Balance box.

BALANCING ACCOUNTS

Figure 9.5 Click each transaction that has cleared on your bank statement in the Reconcile window.

Figure 9.6 Click the OK button in the Reconcile Complete window.

4. Enter the Ending Balance from your bank statement.

5. Enter the amount, date, and category of service charges or interest transactions.

6. Click the Start button to open the Reconcile window (**Figure 9.5**).

7. Click each transaction that has cleared on your bank statement.

   A checkmark appears next to each cleared transaction.

8. Double-click on any transaction in error in the Reconcile window to open the account register and edit it. To add a missing transaction, click the New Transaction button at the bottom of the window to open the account register and make the addition.

9. As you check off each transaction, Quicken updates the "Difference this Statement" figure in the right lower corner of the window. When you've checked off all the transactions, that figure should be zero. If it is, click the Finish button.

   If a difference amount still appears, skip to "Correcting Differences" later in this chapter to find out how to correct the problem.

10. If you balance successfully, the Reconcile Complete window appears (**Figure 9.6**). Click the OK button, and you're done!

✔ Tips

- At the bottom of the Reconcile window (refer to **Figure 9.5**), the "Sort by" pop-up menu lets you sort items in the lists by number or by date.

- Reconciliation problems occur for a variety of reasons, but it's usually because a previous month was not reconciled. See the Quicken User Manual for details on fixing beginning balance problems.

BALANCING ACCOUNTS

To balance a credit card account:

1. Credit card accounts are balanced in almost the same way as checking, savings, or money market accounts. Follow steps 1 through 10 in the preceding section using a credit card account.

2. If you balance successfully, the Reconcile Complete window appears, which looks a bit different for credit card accounts (**Figure 9.7**).

3. If you want a make a payment on your credit card at this time, click the Yes button. The Pay Credit Card Bill window appears (**Figure 9.8**).

4. Select the account you wish to pay from, and then select the means of payment using the Handwritten, Printed, or Electronic radio button.

5. Choose the amount you will pay by selecting the Minimum, Full, or Other radio button. If you select Other, fill in the amount you wish to pay in the box.

6. Click the Pay button.

   Quicken enters the payment in the register for the account you selected. If you wish, Quicken will write a check for the payment (**Figure 9.9**).

Figure 9.7 Just as with your checking account, after you balance your credit card account successfully, the Reconcile Complete window appears.

Figure 9.8 Click the Pay button to make a payment to your credit card account.

Figure 9.9 Quicken will then write a check to pay off your debt.

BALANCING ACCOUNTS

Correcting Differences

In the Reconcile window, if the "Difference this Statement" amount is not zero, it means that your account is not balancing for the current statement period. This usually occurs for one of two reasons: either a wrong number of payment or deposit items have been checked or some of the checked items have incorrect dollar amounts.

To find the mistakes:

1. Count the number of credit items on your bank statement, and then count the number of deposits shown in the Reconcile window. If the number doesn't match, you've found the problem.

   or

   Compare the number of checks and payments on your bank statement against the number of debit items in the Reconcile window.

   You might not have recorded an item in the register, or you might have duplicated a transaction, entered a payment as a deposit or a deposit as a payment, or marked an item cleared by mistake.

2. If the number of items is correct but the statement still doesn't balance, you have a problem with the dollar amount of one or more of your items. By hand or using a calculator, add up all the transactions shown under "Payments and Checks."

3. Compare the total with the total of debits on the statement.

   If the numbers don't match, you have a problem with the dollar amount of the debits.

4. Add up all the transactions shown under "Deposits" and compare them to the total of deposits on the statement.

   If those numbers don't match, there's a discrepancy in your deposit figures.

CORRECTING DIFFERENCES

Letting Quicken fix the problem

If the dollar amount of an unreconciled balance is small, you may decide that it's not worth the time it takes to track down the mistake. In that case, you can let Quicken enter a register adjustment, which will force your account to reconcile.

If you click the Finish button in the Reconcile window while there is still a difference, Quicken will pop up the Adjust Ending Balance window (**Figure 9.10**). If you want Quicken to enter an account adjustment, click the Adjust Register button. If you want to take another whack at finding the mistake, click the Return to Reconcile button.

✔ Tips

- The most common mistake in this area is transposing two digits during data entry.

- If you're off by a fairly small amount that is an even number (for example, $8.00, rather than $3.87), it's likely that you missed entering a bank service charge of some sort. Check your statement carefully for charges you don't normally see, such as those for check printing or using another bank's ATM.

- Using Online Banking (see Chapter 11) makes balancing your checkbook and other accounts even easier, because you download your bank and credit card statements directly into Quicken's account registers.

Figure 9.10 To have Quicken enter a balance adjustment for an account that just won't balance, click the Adjust Register button.

CORRECTING DIFFERENCES

DEALING WITH CREDIT CARDS | 10

Credit cards are an incredibly convenient way to make purchases. They make it easy to buy things now and pay for them later. The price you pay for this convenience, of course, is the interest your credit card company charges as compensation for the loan of its money. And as purchases and interest charges mount, it's all too easy to get to the point where your credit card debt becomes overwhelming.

If you're already at the point where you are uncomfortable with the size of your debt load, you should use Quicken's Debt Reduction Planner to develop a plan to get out of debt. See Chapter 17 for more about the Debt Reduction Planner.

One way to make sure that your credit card debt doesn't spin out of control is to track it carefully on a monthly basis. That means categorizing your card charges so that you know where you're spending your money and reconciling your credit card accounts to make sure that spending doesn't slip by unnoticed.

It's also a good idea to take advantage of Quicken's built-in tools that let you know if you spend more than you want to in a particular category, help you find the best credit card rate, and help you set account limits.

Tracking Credit Card Transactions

Quicken offers two methods for tracking credit cards. The first method is to use the associated register for a credit card account to track each and every transaction separately (**Figure 10.1**). This method lets you see all the transactions within the credit card account, including the current balance; you can create more comprehensive reports about your spending; and it's easier to find and correct data entry errors. However, it does require a little more data entry (although if you arrange to download your credit card statement over the Internet, there's almost no data entry at all).

The other way to handle your credit card transactions is for those of you who always pay your bill in full each month. You would enter the credit card payment into your checking account register, creating a split transaction with a separate line for each purchase you made this month (**Figure 10.2**). This method saves a little bit of data entry and keeps all of your transactions within your checking account. You have to be a little more clever about selecting reports to display your spending, and if you run a balance, you won't be able to track that balance in Quicken; you'll need to refer to your paper statement. You also won't have any easy way to track credits to your credit card account.

I favor the first method of tracking. Sure, it's a bit more data entry, but if I do happen to run a balance for a particular month, I know just what that balance is. And it's much simpler to see where my purchases occurred without having to go into my check register and open each split transaction. Pick a method based on your spending and payment habits, and on the importance of debt tracking in your situation.

Figure 10.1 The best way to handle credit card transactions is to make all your entries in a separate credit card account.

Figure 10.2 Another way to track credit cards is to make payments in your checking account register, creating split transactions to track the categories for your charges.

Figure 10.3 The credit card account button on the tool bar gives you direct access to your credit card account register.

◀	**January 1999**	▶

Su	M	Tu	W	Th	F	Sa
					1	2
3	4	5	6	7	8	9
10	11	12	13	14	15	16
17	18	19	20	21	22	23
24	25	26	27	28	29	30
31						

Figure 10.4 This pop-up calendar makes it easy to select a transaction date.

To enter a credit card transaction in a credit card account:

1. Click the button for your credit card register on the tool bar (**Figure 10.3**), or choose Lists > Registers > *Credit card register* from the menu to open the credit card account register.

2. If the credit card account you want isn't displayed, scroll the account tabs below the register until the account is visible, and then click that tab to display the register.

3. The credit card account register appears (refer to **Figure 10.1**) with the current date filled in and the Date field highlighted. You can change the date by typing in a new date or by clicking the calendar icon underneath the date (**Figure 10.4**).

4. Press the [Tab] key to move to the Ref# field. This is usually unused in a credit card account (you might see a reference number entered here if you download your credit card statement), so press [Tab] again to move to the Payee field.

5. Enter the payee (for a charge) or the name of your credit card company (for a payment).

6. Enter the charge or payment amount.

7. Assign a category to the transaction by typing it into the Category field. The QuickFill feature fills in the category name from the pop-up menu after you enter the first few letters.

   or

   Use the pop-up menu in the Category field to select the category.

8. Enter a memo about the transaction (optional).

9. Click the Enter button (or press the [Enter] key on the keyboard).

   Quicken saves the transaction and adds it to the register (refer to **Figure 10.1**).

TRACKING CREDIT CARD TRANSACTIONS

To enter credit card transactions in your checking account register:

1. Open the checking account register.

2. Enter the date, the check number, the name of your credit card company, and the total payment amount.

3. Click the Split button in the register. The Split Transaction window appears. Enter each charge to your account in the split lines.

4. Enter the category for the first charge in the first Category field in the split, either by typing in the category or by choosing it from the pop-up menu.

5. Type the name of the store or merchant in the first Memo field. If needed, also enter a description of the charge here.

6. Type the amount of the charge in the first Amount field. Quicken subtracts that amount from the total and puts the remainder in the next Amount field.

7. Enter the next category, merchant, and amount on the next line. Repeat this until you have allocated the entire payment or deposit amount and there is no unallocated figure remaining at the bottom of the amount column (refer to **Figure 10.2**). Click the Record button to save the transaction, which is now properly allocated to multiple categories.

Figure 10.5 Start setting credit card limits in the Account List.

Figure 10.6 Update your credit card limit in this window.

Controlling Credit Card Debt

Credit card debt is a particularly troubling form of debt; that piece of plastic is so easy to use that your level of debt can creep up without you even noticing it, and it is only rarely for the kind of goods and services that can be considered investments. Furthermore, the interest rates on cards tend to be extremely high.

If you have entered a credit limit for your card, Quicken's credit card account registers show both the current balance and the Credit Remaining at the bottom. It is easy to see when you are approaching your limit, and when the Credit Remaining figure goes into the red (literally), you know it's time to take urgent action.

To enter your credit limit for a credit card account:

1. Choose Lists > Accounts. The Accounts list opens (**Figure 10.5**).

2. Click a credit card account to select it.

3. Click the Edit button at the bottom of the Account list window.

   The Edit Account window appears (**Figure 10.6**).

4. Enter the credit limit, and then click Done.

✔ Tip

■ One way to control your credit card debt is not to spend as much for debt service. That means using Quicken.com to find the best interest rates on credit cards; there's no reason to spend more money than necessary on interest. See Chapter 19 for more information on using Quicken.com.

Controlling Debt by Budgeting

Perhaps the most useful tools Quicken offers for controlling debt—and credit card debt in particular—are the Budget and Budget Monitoring functions. Obviously, spending more money than you are taking in is going to drive you deeper into debt, and, more than likely, that means more and more dependence on credit cards. Using Quicken, you can set up both an overall budget for your accounts and individual budgets for specific categories and accounts.

QuickBudget uses the data in your file to set up a starting point that you can then modify.

To set up a budget:

1. Choose Activities > Budgeting > Budget Setup or click the Budget button on the tool bar.

   The Create Budget window opens (**Figure 10.7**).

2. Select the radio button for Use QuickBudget... to open the QuickBudget window (**Figure 10.8**).

Figure 10.7 The Create Budget window sets up the categories for your budget.

Figure 10.8 The QuickBudget option makes it easy to get the process started.

Figure 10.9 The Budget Setup window is a little intimidating at first, but easily managed.

3. You can probably leave the settings as they are for the first pass, so click OK. Then Click Create in the Create Budget window. The Budget Setup window (**Figure 10.9**) opens with a long column of figures, many of them zeros.

4. Click any line to edit it by typing a new figure in the field that opens. You can delete the line by choosing Edit > Delete Item From Budget or by pressing ⌘D. When you are done, you can close the window by clicking in the close box in the upper left corner.

5. You can create additional budgets using these steps by choosing New Budget from the pop-up menu in the upper left of the window.

✔ Tip

- By setting up very specific budgets—for example, areas where you tend to over-spend for discretional items like clothing, dining, and entertainment—you can keep a tight rein on your spending habits.

Using the Budget Monitor to track your expenditures

The Budget Monitor is a bar graph that shows how well you are sticking to your budget in the current period.

To use Budget Monitoring:

1. Choose Activities > Budgeting > Budget Monitoring, or click the Monitor button (**Figure 10.10**) on the tool bar.

The Budget Monitoring window opens (**Figure 10.11**).

2. From the Pop-up menus across the top of the window, choose the budget and time period you want to look.

3. Click the Set Up Monitoring button at the bottom left corner of the window.

The Set Up Monitoring window (**Figure 10.12**) opens.

4. Select the categories or category groups you want to view, and then click OK.

The Monitoring window will display a bar for each category or group chosen. The bars are colored green for Good, yellow for Caution, red for Danger.

5. Position the cursor over one of the bars and hold down the mouse button. The dollar figure for the category appears (**Figure 10.13**).

Figure 10.10 Click the Monitor button to open the Budget Monitor.

Figure 10.11 The Budget Monitoring window shows how well you are keeping to your budget.

Figure 10.12 The Set Up Monitoring screen controls which categories are displayed.

Figure 10.13 You can read the dollar figures for each bar by holding down the mouse button over it.

CONTROLLING DEBT BY BUDGETING

BANKING AND PAYING BILLS ONLINE

Using your computer to download bank statements and pay bills is a new and, to some people, a scary way of dealing with your bank. Yet it can save you a lot of time and a bit of money.

Doing your banking online can save you time because you don't need to hand record your checks, ATM withdrawals, or credit card transactions. Instead, you download them from your bank, review the transactions to catch any possible errors and make sure they are properly categorized, and then add them to your account registers with the click of a button. Because the information is current as of the close of the previous banking day, you can monitor your cash flow more closely. This lets you make sure, for example, that deposits are credited to your account before you write checks and helps you to avoid expensive bounced check charges.

Online bill payment lets you transfer money from your checking account directly to your creditors. You don't have to write or print checks, stuff envelopes, find stamps, or go to the post office. You simply enter a payment in an account register and have Quicken send it over the phone lines.

Setting Up Online Banking

To use online banking, you must first have access to the Internet. You'll need an Internet Service Provider (ISP) and a modem or another connection to the Internet. You need to tell Quicken what sort of Internet connection you have. Additionally, if you tell Quicken which Web browser you're using, Quicken can use the browser to show you information on Intuit's Web site about how to apply for online banking.

To set Quicken's Internet preferences:

1. Choose Edit > Preferences to open the Preferences window (**Figure 11.1**). Then select the Internet icon from the scrolling list on the left.

2. Select the ISP you're using, either America Online or another ISP.

3. Click the Select Browser button.
   The Open window appears (**Figure 11.2**).

4. Select the Web browser that you use, and then click the Open button.

5. Click the OK button to save your Internet preferences.

Figure 11.1 Select the Internet icon from the scrolling list on the left of the Preferences window.

Figure 11.2 Select the appropriate browser in the open file window.

Figure 11.3 Quicken.com provides a wealth of useful information when you're shopping for an institution that offers online banking—or even just considering the option.

Applying for Online Banking

You must contact your bank or other financial institution to get online access for checking, savings, and credit card accounts. Not all financial institutions support online banking, and some support online banking only for certain account types, such as checking but not credit card accounts. Even if your financial institution doesn't support online banking, you can still use online bill payment through Intuit. If you have accounts at more than one financial institution, you'll need to apply to each one separately.

Each financial institution sets its own fees for online banking. The fee amount varies from bank to bank, so it's a good idea to shop around for the best deal. You can find the most complete list of banks and their online banking fees on Intuit's Web site at http://www.quicken.com. Look for the Banking & Credit section, and then look for Intuit banking partners. You can also access the list from within Quicken 2000, by choosing Online > Financial Institutions (see **Figure 11.3**).

After you have signed up for online banking, your financial institution will send you a kit with information to help you set up your Quicken accounts for online banking. You'll also receive an initial personal identification number (PIN), which you should change in your first online banking session.

APPLYING FOR ONLINE BANKING

To enable a Quicken account for online use:

1. Choose Online > Enable Online Banking > Online Banking.

   The Select Account to Enable window appears (**Figure 11.4**).

2. Select the account you want to set up for online service, and then click OK.

   The Enable Online Banking window appears (**Figure 11.5**).

3. Click the "Enable direct account access" check box if you'll be using this account to download statements. Click the "Enable direct online payment" check box to use the account for bill payments.

4. Refer to the information kit you received from your financial institution to enter the financial institution name, routing number, account number, account type, and Customer ID, exactly as listed in the kit.

5. Enter your Social Security number.

6. Click the Save button. You return to the Select Account to Enable window, which now shows a lightning bolt next to the account name, which indicates that it is enabled for online services.

7. Repeat steps 2 through 6 to enable other accounts.

Online-enabled accounts

Figure 11.4 Select the account you want to set up for online service.

Figure 11.5 Check the boxes to enable electronic banking and fill in the form below.

Figure 11.6 Click the Download button to open the Download Transactions window.

Financial institution pop-up menu

Accept items button

Last online balance

Account pop-up menu

Figure 11.7 Start your online transaction from the Download Transactions window.

Figure 11.8 Enter your PIN and click the OK button.

Going Online

The first time that you go online, it's a good idea to just download your current transactions. This gets you used to the process and lets you update your account registers. During this first session, your bank may prompt you to change your PIN.

To download transactions:

1. Click the Download button in the tool bar (**Figure 11.6**), or choose Online > Download Transactions.

   The Download Transactions window appears (**Figure 11.7**).

2. If you have online accounts at more than one financial institution, choose the financial institution you want from the pop-up menu below the institution's logo on the left side of the window.

3. Click the Get Online Data button.

   Quicken connects to the Internet and then asks for your PIN (**Figure 11.8**).

4. Enter your PIN, and then click the OK button.

   (continued)

5. Review the information in the Online Transmission Summary window (**Figure 11.9**), and then click OK.

Quicken displays the downloaded transactions in the top half of the Download Transactions window. You can sort the downloaded transactions by clicking one of the column titles.

Quicken compares the downloaded transactions with transactions that are already in your account register. If the transactions correspond, the word "Match" appears next to the downloaded transaction in the Download Transaction window.

6. Click each matched transaction to place a checkmark next to it, signifying that it is ready to be cleared in your register.

If Quicken doesn't find a match for a downloaded transaction, the transaction appears in the list in the Status column marked "New." Quicken marks a transaction as New when you haven't yet entered that transaction in your account register or when the check number or amount differs from the transaction that you entered.

Figure 11.9 Review the information in the Online Transmission Summary window and then click OK.

7. For these New transactions, you'll need to enter the missing payee and/or category information. Select the New transaction in the transaction list.

   Quicken displays the transaction in the register at the bottom of the Download Transactions window.

8. Make your changes in the register, and then click the Record button. The transaction's status will change to "Match." Click the newly matched transaction to place a checkmark next to it.

9. Repeat steps 7 and 8 for every New transaction.

10. Click the Accept ✓ Items button.

    Quicken adds the checked items to the account register marked cleared and removes them from the transaction list in the Download Transactions window.

✔ Tips

- Your financial institution may label ATM transactions and service charges as EFT, which stands for Electronic Funds Transfer.

- Quicken doesn't close the Internet connection after it finishes downloading, so if you're using a dial-up connection with a modem, you must close it manually.

- You can edit your transactions to change the category either before or after updating your register, but it's usually easier to do it in the Download Transactions window.

Is Online Banking Secure?

Since online banking and online bill payment transactions travel over the Internet, it's perfectly reasonable to wonder if your financial data can be intercepted and used by criminals. Quicken's security measures make it extremely unlikely.

The first line of defense is the Personal Identification Number (PIN) that you must enter whenever you use online banking or bill payment. When you first sign up for online banking, your bank sends you a PIN that you can (and should) change. After you change it, you're the only one who knows that PIN. For extra security, you should change your PIN on a regular basis.

For additional security, Quicken encrypts all transferred information—back and forth. Encryption is a technique that scrambles data before it is sent using a mathematical algorithm. At the other end, your bank unscrambles the data. (For those more technically inclined, Quicken uses 128-bit DES [Data Encryption Standard] encryption along with SSL [Secure Sockets Layer] transfer protocols.)

GOING ONLINE

Paying Bills Online

To make online bill payments with Quicken, you'll first need to set up the payment recipients in the Payee list. To send a payment, you just select a payee from the list, create the payment instruction, and send it to your financial institution.

To set up a payee:

1. Choose Online > Payments > Online Payees or select Online Payees from the EPay menu on the Banking section of the tool bar.

   The Payees window appears (**Figure 11.10**).

2. Click the New button.

   The Set Up Payee window appears (**Figure 11.11**).

3. Enter the payee's name, address, and phone number.

4. Enter the account number that the payee uses to identify you. If the payee doesn't use account numbers, enter your name.

5. Click the Create button. Quicken will present a dialog box asking you to review and verify the payee information. If it is correct, click the Yes button; otherwise, click the No button and correct the payee information.

   After you verify the information, Quicken adds the new payee to the Payee list.

Figure 11.10 Click the New button to open the Set Up Payee window.

Figure 11.11 Enter the payee's information and account number.

Figure 11.12 Click the EPay button in the Banking section of the tool bar to open the Enter Online Payment window.

Figure 11.13 The Enter Online Payment window looks like a check. Fill it in with QuickFill's help.

Figure 11.14 Click the Out Box button in the tool bar to open the Out Box.

Figure 11.15 Review the items in the Out Box and click Send Now.

To create and send an online payment:

1. Open the register you want to use to make the payment.

2. Use the EPay button in the Banking section of the tool bar (**Figure 11.12**) to select Enter Payment or choose Online > Payments > Enter Payment from the menu. The Enter Online Payment window appears (**Figure 11.13**).

3. Choose Online > Payments > Online Payees to open the Payees window.

4. In the Payees window, select one of the payees, and then click the Use button. The payee's name is transferred to the Enter Online Payment window.

5. Fill in the amount and the category of the payment in the Enter Online Payment window.

6. If you plan to create more online payments in the current session, click the Put in Out Box button. Quicken stores the payment in a list of instructions to send to your financial institution the next time you connect. If this is the only payment you are making, you can click the Send Now button and Quicken immediately connects online, prompts you for your PIN, and sends your payment instruction.

7. If you put payments into the Out Box, click the Out Box button in the Banking section of the tool bar (**Figure 11.14**). The Out Box appears (**Figure 11.15**).

8. Review the items in the Out Box, and if you're satisfied, click the Send Now button. Quicken connects to your financial institution and sends the payments.

(continued)

✔ Tips

■ If your payee is set up to receive electronic funds transfers, payment is transferred directly from your account to your payee's account. This usually takes less than two business days. If the payee doesn't accept EFTs, your financial institution prints a check and sends it to the payee by US mail. It's important that you allow sufficient time for the payment to get to the payee to avoid a late charge. So make sure that you schedule payments at least three or four days before a payment due date.

■ Don't forget that a payee will often need a day or two after receiving a check to process the payment and credit your account.

Why not use the Web?

Some banks now allow you to view accounts and make transactions over the World Wide Web, rather than download transactions into Quicken. Web access is nice for quick checks of account balances, but it's inferior to downloading into Quicken. Why? The main reason is speed. The Web way is slo-o-o-o-w. And if you view information on the Web using your Web browser, you still have the problem of entering that data into your registers. On the other hand, downloading a month's worth of transactions into Quicken takes less than a minute. The direct download method works much better.

12

CREATING REPORTS

I have to admit that before I started using Quicken, my financial house was not exactly in order. Like many people, I had built up a bit too much credit card debt; I balanced my checkbook twice a year, whether it needed it or not; and although I knew that money was coming in and money was going out, I didn't know just where all that money was going.

Quicken's reports, one of its most powerful tools, went a long way toward solving my financial problems by giving me a comprehensive picture of my finances. After using Quicken for just a few months, I had a good record of how much I was spending and where I was spending it. I could also see how much I was spending on interest, which really gave me the impetus to pay off those bills.

One of the best features of Quicken reports is that you can use them to look at your financial data in different ways. You can view your finances in as much or as little detail as you need, and you can pull out just the information that you want. For example, at tax time, I pull a report to show all of my tax-deductible expenditures for the previous year, all neatly categorized and totaled. My accountant appreciates it (anything would be better than that shoe box of loose receipts I use to drop on his desk), and because using the reports takes less of his time, it saves me money.

Using Reports

Quicken comes with a variety of report templates that cover most of the questions you have about your finances. You can customize those reports to zero in on just the information that you want.

You can get six kinds of reports from Quicken: EasyAnswer reports, QuickReports, Standard reports, Memorized reports, Shortcut reports, and Register and List reports.

You use a slightly different method to create each kind of report. You can move among different kinds of reports by using the tabs at the top of the Reports window. The scrolling window at the left side of the window displays the names of Quicken's report templates. When you click on the name of a report template, Quicken shows you a sample of that report on the right side of the Reports window.

Figure 12.1 Click the Reports button in the tool bar to open the Reports window.

Figure 12.2 The Reports window gives you access to a wide variety of report templates.

Figure 12.3 EasyAnswer reports offer quick and basic information about your finances.

Figure 12.4 An example of a Quicken report.

Using EasyAnswer Reports

EasyAnswer reports give you quick answers to eight basic questions, such as "Where did I spend my money?" and "What are my investments worth?"

To create an EasyAnswer report:

1. Click the Reports button in the tool bar (**Figure 12.1**), or choose Activities > Reports & Graphs > Reports to open the Reports window (**Figure 12.2**).

2. Click on the EasyAnswer tab. Quicken displays the EasyAnswer report window (**Figure 12.3**). This window shows eight basic questions that you can ask about your finances. Select the radio button with the question that you want to ask.

3. If necessary, adjust the date range by choosing a new time frame from the pop-up menu next to the radio button that you clicked.

4. If you picked a question that requires it, choose a category to narrow your report from the pop-up menu next to the question.

5. Click the Create button. Quicken displays the report on your screen (**Figure 12.4**).

USING EASYANSWER REPORTS

Using QuickReport

A QuickReport is a transaction detail report that offers only a few options; it's designed to give you fast information for one specific payee, category, account, or security.

To create a QuickReport:

1. Click the QuickReport button in the tool bar (**Figure 12.5**) to open the Create QuickReport dialog box (**Figure 12.6**).

2. Choose the source for the report using the pop-up menu. Your choices are Payee & Description, Category, Class, Memo, Account, or Security.

3. Type in your search criteria.

4. Choose the date range for the QuickReport from the pop-up menu next to Date.

5. Click the OK button. Quicken grinds through its data file and presents a transaction report based on your criteria (**Figure 12.7**).

Figure 12.5 Click the QuickReport button in the task bar to open the QuickReport dialog box.

Figure 12.6 Enter information in the Create QuickReport dialog box for fast report results.

Figure 12.7 A transaction report created with the QuickReport feature. In this report, we searched for all transactions from last year-to-date where the category was Household.

USING QUICKREPORT

—*Magnifying-glass cursor*

Figure 12.8 When the cursor turns into a magnifying glass, you can zoom in for more detailed information by double-clicking.

Figure 12.9 The detail transaction report produced by zooming in on a category—in this case, Fun.

Figure 12.10 Zooming further, the final level of detail shows the original transaction in the account register.

Zooming in on the Details

You can use QuickZoom to examine the information in your reports in greater detail. If you're viewing a report that summarizes the amounts from a category, you can double-click on an amount and QuickZoom will take you to another report that shows more detail about the item you selected. But if you use QuickZoom in a transaction report, Quicken opens the register and shows you the original transaction.

To use QuickZoom:

1. Create a report summarizing expenses by category. (That's just an example; you can actually create any sort of report you wish.)

2. In the open report window, move the cursor over one of the amounts in the report until the cursor turns into a magnifying glass (**Figure 12.8**).

3. Double-click on the amount of a category. A new transaction report window opens showing you the detailed transactions for the category (**Figure 12.9**).

4. To view an original transaction, double-click on an amount in the detailed transaction report window. The account register for the transaction will open, with the transaction selected (**Figure 12.10**).

Using Standard Reports

Standard reports give you basic information, such as details of transactions, net worth, and category transaction reports. In the tabs at the top of the Reports window, Quicken lists Standard, Business, and Investment report types. All three of these types are generated in the same fashion.

To create a Standard report:

1. Click the Reports button in the tool bar, or choose Activities > Reports & Graphs > Reports to open the Reports window (**Figure 12.11**).

2. Click on the Standard, Business, or Investment tabs at the top of the Reports window. The window will switch to the area you clicked.

3. In the scrolling pane on the left side of the window, select a template for a report that you want to create. On the right side of the window, Quicken shows you a sample of the kind of report you select.

4. If necessary, change the date range of the report by changing the value of the Date pop-up menu or by typing in a date or dates in the date field in the Reports window.

5. Click the Create button to generate the report (**Figure 12.12**).

Figure 12.11 You can change the date range of a report by typing in a new date or by choosing a new value in the Date pop-up menu.

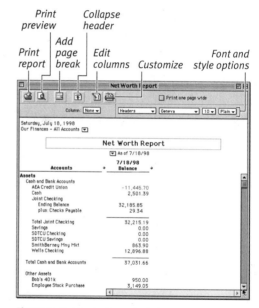

Figure 12.12 A typical report window.

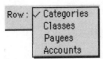

Figure 12.13 Select an option from the Row pop-up menu to change the contents of the rows in a report.

Figure 12.14 Select an option from the Column pop-up menu to choose the contents of the columns in the report.

Figure 12.15 These pop-up menus let you change the look of the text in each part of a report.

Add page break   Collapse header   Edit columns

Figure 12.16 Use these icons to customize the overall look of the report.

Figure 12.17 The Edit Columns window lets you choose which columns to include in your report.

Customizing Reports

You can customize reports in Quicken in two ways: by creating a custom layout of a Standard report or by creating an entirely new custom report.

To customize report layouts:

1. Follow steps 1 through 6 in the previous section, "To create a Standard report."

2. In the Report window, choose one or more of the following formatting options:

◆ Change the contents of the rows in a report by choosing from the Row pop-up menu (**Figure 12.13**).

◆ Choose the contents of the columns in the report by selecting an option from the Column pop-up menu (**Figure 12.14**).

◆ Change the look of the text in the report with the font, font size, and style pop-up menus (**Figure 12.15**).

◆ Click the "Print one page wide" check box to resize the report to fit on one page.

◆ Edit the report title by selecting it and typing in a new one.

◆ Resize the width of the columns in the report by clicking and dragging the diamonds between each column head. Drag the rules under each column head to rearrange the columns in the report.

✔ Tip

■ You can also customize the look of the report by clicking on one of the three icons in the Report window (**Figure 12.16**). To add a page break, select a row in the report and click on the Page Break icon. Click on the Collapse Header icon to remove the header from the printed document. Click on the Edit Columns icon to open a window that allows you to select which columns to include in your report (**Figure 12.17**).

To create a custom report:

1. Follow steps 1 through 4 in "To create a Standard report" to choose a report template.

2. Click the Customize button at the bottom of the Reports window. The Customize Report window appears.

3. Make changes in one or more of the following areas:

◆ The Layout tab (**Figure 12.18**) of the Customize Report window lets you specify row and column headings as well as the date range for the report.

◆ The Content tab lets you choose which information will appear in the report. (**Figure 12.19**). You can narrow the focus of your report to show only the items of your interest.

◆ The Organization tab (**Figure 12.20**) allows you to organize the look of a report either as an income and expense report or by cash flow.

Figure 12.18 The Layout tab lets you set the basic report parameters.

Figure 12.19 Narrow the report's information from the Content tab.

Figure 12.20 The Organization tab lets you switch between two different ways to view you report.

Figure 12.21 Enter the name of a memorized report in the Memorize Report Template window.

Figure 12.22 Choose a report that you have already memorized from the Memorized tab in the Reports window.

Using Memorized Reports

Tweaking reports until they're just the way that you want them can take some effort, and it would be a waste of your time if you had to re-create a custom report every time. Instead, you can save custom settings and reuse them. These are called Memorized reports.

To memorize a report:

1. Create a custom report.

2. Choose Edit > Memorize, or press ⌘M. The Memorize Report Template window appears (**Figure 12.21**).

3. Enter a name and a description for the report. If you click the "Use current date" check box, Quicken will create future reports using the current date, rather than the dates that you specified when you customized the report.

4. Click the Memorize button.

To use a memorized report:

1. Click the Reports button in the task bar.

2. In the Reports window, click on the Memorized tab (**Figure 12.22**).

3. Click on the memorized report that you want to use. Optionally, change the date range at the bottom of the Reports window.

4. Click the Create button.

Using Shortcut Reports

Shortcut reports are found in the account registers. They are simple year-to-date transaction reports of all occurrences of a selected payee or category.

To create a shortcut report:

1. Open an account register.

2. Scroll through the register until you find the transaction on which you want a report. Click on the transaction to select it.

3. When you selected the transaction, the Shortcuts pop-up menu appeared in that transaction (**Figure 12.23**). Click on the Shortcuts menu, and choose either "Report on [payee name]" or "Report on [category name]." Quicken generates the report (**Figure 12.24**).

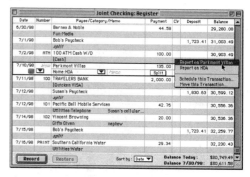

Figure 12.23 The Shortcuts pop-up menu in the account register lets you get fast reports on a transaction.

Figure 12.24 The Transaction Detail Shortcuts Report gives you quick year-to-date information about the payee or category of a transaction.

Figure 12.25 To print any type of Quicken report, choose File > Report or click the Print button at the top of the Reports window, and click Print.

Printing Reports

Quicken makes it easy to print reports and lists of all kinds, whether from the Reports section or from other areas of the program, such as account registers or lists.

To print a report:

1. Click the Reporting button in the activity bar.

2. Click the Reports button in the task bar to open the Reports window.

3. Create a standard or memorized report as described earlier in this chapter, or choose an existing report.

4. Choose File > Print Report. The printer dialog box will appear.

   or

   Click the Print button at the top of the Reports window. The printer dialog box will appear, as shown in **Figure 12.25**.

5. Click the Print button to print your report.

✔ Tip

■ Note that Quicken, unlike almost every other Macintosh program, doesn't use ⌘P as the shortcut key for its printing needs. That shortcut key is reserved for Print Checks.

Register and List Reports

These aren't exactly reports in the same sense as the the the other five types. With these reports, Quicken simply allows you to print the current list or account register. But sometimes that's all you need.

To print an account register or a list:

1. Open the account register or list that you want to print.

2. If you're printing a register, choose File > Print Register (**Figure 12.26**). The Print Register window will appear (**Figure 12.27**). Enter the date range of the register entries you wish to print, then click the OK button. If you are printing a list, the menu item will be called File > Print [*List Name*] ([*List Name*] is the name of the list you have open.)

3. The printer dialog box will appear.

4. Click the Print button.

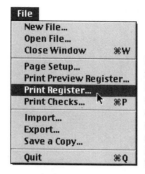

Figure 12.26 Sometimes it's handy to have a hard copy of all or part of a transactions register. That's easily accomplished, simply by choosing Print Register from the File menu.

Figure 12.27 You can print out an entire history of your transactions from a given register, or specify a range of dates, using the two pop-up calendars or entering the dates in the windows.

13

CREATING GRAPHS

When it comes to getting a good overview of your finances, reports are good but graphs are better. Graphs can often illustrate relationships in your finances that numeric reports don't make clear.

Quicken can display your financial data as bar graphs, line graphs, and pie charts to help you quickly analyze your income and expenses, develop budgets, and determine your net worth.

In addition to their informational benefits, graphs can give you an important emotional boost, as I discovered while working to pay off my consumer debt. I created a bar graph that showed how much debt I owed. Every month, as I made payments, I'd check the graph to see how much the debt bar had shrunk. It felt great to see the downward trend in graphic form as I worked toward my goals—and it felt even better the month that the bar finally hit the zero mark.

As with reports (see Chapter 12 for more about reports), Quicken comes with a variety of templates to get you started using graphs. You can create custom graphs to answer particular questions about your finances. Quicken has three main types of graphs: EasyAnswer graphs, Standard graphs, and Memorized graphs.

Using EasyAnswer Graphs

EasyAnswer graphs address basic questions about your finances.

To create an EasyAnswer graph:

1. Click the Graphs button in the Reporting section of the tool bar (**Figure 13.1**). The Graphs window appears (**Figure 13.2**).

2. Click on the EasyAnswer tab. Quicken shows you the EasyAnswer Graphs window (**Figure 13.3**).

3. Select the radio button to indicate the question that you want to ask.

4. If necessary, choose a new time frame from the pop-up menu next to the radio button that you clicked.

5. If your question requires a category selection, choose one from the pop-up menu next to the selected question.

6. Click the Create button. Quicken displays the graph on your screen (**Figure 13.4**).

Figure 13.1 Click this button to open the Graphs window.

Figure 13.2 You create all of your graphs in Quicken from the Graphs window.

Figure 13.3 Use the EasyAnswer Graphs screen to get fast financial graphs.

Figure 13.4 Quicken displays a completed graph.

USING EASYANSWER GRAPHS

Figure 13.5 Click and hold down the mouse button when the cursor becomes a magnifying glass to see the dollar value of the graph segment.

Figure 13.6 Double-click on the graph segment to open a more detailed graph.

Figure 13.7 Double-click on the detailed to see a report showing you the original transactions that were used to create the graph.

To use QuickZoom to get details:

1. Move the cursor over one of the colored areas on an existing graph. The cursor will turn into a magnifying glass. Click and hold the mouse button to see the dollar value of that segment of the graph (**Figure 13.5**).

2. Double-click on a segment of the graph to open another graph showing you more detail (**Figure 13.6**).

3. For even more detail, double-click on a segment of the detailed graph. A report window opens, showing you the original transactions that make up the graph segment (**Figure 13.7**).

USING EASYANSWER GRAPHS

Using a Standard Graph

Standard graphs provide such information as your net worth, the value of your investment portfolio, and details about your income and expenses. You can customize Standard graphs to suit your own needs.

To create a Standard graph:

1. Click the Graphs button in the tool bar to open the Graphs window.

2. Click on the Standard tab.

   Quicken shows you the Standard Graphs window (**Figure 13.8**).

3. Select the type of graph that you want to create.

4. If necessary, change the date range of the graph by changing the value of the Date pop-up menu, or by typing in a date or dates in the date fields in the Standard Graphs window.

5. Click the Create button to generate the graph (**Figure 13.9**).

✔ Tip

■ Use QuickZoom with any type of graph to view more detailed information about your finances.

Figure 13.8 Quicken provides a variety of standard graphs.

Figure 13.9 You can customize a standard income and expense graph to suit your needs.

Figure 13.10 Hold down the mouse button when the cursor becomes a magnifying glass to see your Net Worth graph, which shows your current net worth dollar value.

Creating a Net Worth Graph

Net Worth graphs are a bit complicated. Your net worth is calculated by subtracting your liabilities from your assets. These bar graphs show your assets above the zero line and your liabilities below the zero line, with your net worth showing as a small red square (hopefully above the zero line!).

To create a Net Worth graph:

1. Click the Graphs button in the tool bar to open the Graphs window.

2. Click on the Standard tab.
   Quicken shows you the Standard Graphs window.

3. Select the Net Worth template on the Standard tab.

4. If necessary, change the date range.

5. Click the Create button.
   Quicken generates your Net Worth graph (**Figure 13.10**).

Customizing Graphs

Quicken's standard graph templates are adequate in most cases, but you'll sometimes want to create a custom graph to get some specific information. For example, you might want to compare your income against your spouse's income, or (if you're really looking for marital trouble) compare your expenses.

Figure 13.11 You can customize your graphs from this window.

To create a custom graph:

1. Click the Graphs button on the Reporting section of the tool bar.

2. Click on the EasyAnswer or Standard tab in the Graphs window, and then select the kind of graph you wish to create.

3. Click the Customize button.

   The Customize Graph window appears (**Figure 13.11**).

4. Click on the Layout tab. If you wish, change the title and date range of the graph.

5. Click on the Content tab. Use the pop-up menus to narrow the scope of the graph.

6. Click the OK button to create your custom graph.

✔ Tips

- If you have already created a graph, you can customize it by clicking the Customize button in the lower left corner of the Graphs window.

- If you decide you don't like the changes that you made in the Customize Graph window, click the Defaults button to return all the settings back to their initial values.

Figure 13.12 After you have customized a graph, you can memorize it and give it a name.

Figure 13.13 Choose a previously memorized report from the Memorized tab.

Using Memorized Graphs

Once you have customized a graph, chances are you're going to want to use it again. Memorized graphs are custom graphs that you have saved for later reuse.

To memorize a graph:

1. Create a custom graph as described above.

2. Choose Edit > Memorize or press ⌘Ⓜ. The Memorize Graph Template dialog box appears (**Figure 13.12**).

3. Enter a name and a description for the graph. If you click the "Use current date" check box, Quicken will create future graphs using the current date, rather than the dates that you specified when you customized the graph.

4. Click the Memorize button.

To use a memorized graph:

1. Click the Graphs button in the tool bar.

2. In the Graphs window, click on the Memorized tab (**Figure 13.13**). Select a graph that you previously memorized. Optionally, change the date range at the bottom of the Graphs window to see information pertaining to a particular range.

3. Click the Create button.

To delete a memorized graph:

1. Click the Graphs button in the tool bar.

2. In the Graphs window, click on the Memorized tab. Select a graph that you previously memorized.

3. Choose Edit > Delete Graph, or press ⌘Ⓓ.

4. Click the Yes button when Quicken asks you to confirm the deletion.

Printing Graphs

Most of the time, you'll be displaying your graphs onscreen, but on occasion you'll want to print them out to show others. You might want to print an income graph to dazzle a loan officer, for example, or to demonstrate to your doubting parents what a financial whiz you've become.

To print a graph or chart:

1. Open or create a graph or chart.

2. Choose File > Print Graph (**Figure 13.14**). The printer dialog box appears.

3. Click the Print button to print the graph or chart.

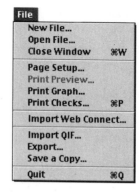

Figure 13.14 You can print any type of Quicken graph simply by choosing Print Graph from the File menu while the graph is displayed on screen.

WORKING WITH LOANS AND MORTGAGES

Loans come in two flavors: either you are borrowing money from another person or from a financial institution, or, perhaps a happier sort, you are lending money to someone else. Quicken handles both kinds of loans with aplomb, creating an account for each new loan.

When you are borrowing money, Quicken tracks how the loan is *amortized*, or paid off, to show you the interest you are paying, the remaining principal, and the length and amounts of your payment schedule. When you set up this kind of loan, Quicken automatically creates a liability account.

When you loan money to someone else, Quicken sets up a payment schedule and creates an asset account.

Creating Loans

To set up a loan account, Quicken needs information about the terms of the loan and the lender or borrower. Then Quicken creates the loan payment schedule and the principal asset or liability account.

Figure 14.1 Click the Loans button to begin creating a loan.

Figure 14.2 The Loans window shows the loans you've entered and lets you start a new loan account.

To create a loan
(when you're the borrower):

1. Click the Loans button in the Assets & Debt section of the tool bar (**Figure 14.1**) or select Lists > Loans.

   The Loans window appears (**Figure 14.2**).

2. Click the New button.

   The Loan Interview window appears (**Figure 14.3**).

3. Select the radio buttons in the Loan Interview window as appropriate for the loan that you're creating.

4. Click the Continue button to open the Set Up Loan window (**Figure 14.4**).

5. In the Set Up Loan window, enter the name of your lender.

6. Enter the payment amounts. Enter your monthly (or quarterly, annual, etc.) payment in the Principal + Interest field. If you're creating a real estate loan and extra fees are added to the loan, such as PMI, property taxes, etc., enter those amounts too.

7. Enter the date of your first payment.

8. Indicate the frequency of the payment. If this loan will be paid on a schedule other than monthly (the default), change the setting of the Frequency pop-up menu.

9. Enter the total number of payments.

Figure 14.3 Quicken learns about the kind of loan that you want to set up in the Loan Interview window.

Figure 14.4 You'll enter most of your loan information in the Set Up Loan window.

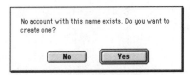

Figure 14.5 Quicken confirms that you want to set up a new liability account.

Figure 14.6 The Preview Payment window lets you make sure that your loan is set up correctly before the final creation step occurs.

10. Enter the annual interest rate.

11. Choose an expense category to track the interest paid on the loan.

12. Enter a name for the principal liability account that you'll use to track this loan. Quicken pops up a dialog box confirming that you want to create a new liability account (**Figure 14.5**).

13. Click the Yes button.

14. Enter the total loan amount.

15. In the Payment Options area, click the "Confirm payment before recording" check box if any of these conditions apply:
    ◆ You want to review or change the payment information every time you make a payment.
    ◆ You plan to make prepayments to reduce your principal and pay off the loan faster.
    ◆ The loan has a variable interest rate.

16. Click "Schedule payment on Calendar" if you want to be automatically reminded about your loan payment.

17. To make sure that everything looks good before you finish creating the loan, click the Preview Payment button to open the Preview Payment window (**Figure 14.6**).

18. After you've viewed the information, click the OK button to return to the Set Up Loan window.

19. If the loan information looked OK, click the Create button. (If not, make your corrections now.)

    If you clicked the "Schedule payment on Calendar" check box, the Calendar window will open to let you schedule your payment. (See Chapter 7 for information on the Financial Calendar.) Your new loan should appear in the Loans window.

To view your payment schedule:

1. Choose Lists > Loans, or click the Loans button in the tool bar, to open the Loans window.

2. In the Loans window, click once on the loan for which you want to see a payment schedule.

3. Click the Payment Schedule button in the Loans window.

   The Payment Schedule window for that loan appears (**Figure 14.7**).

✔ Tips

- The term of a loan must be at least 12 months for Quicken to be able to calculate the interest, principal, and payment information.

- For variable-rate loans, you can change the interest rate when you make a payment or whenever your loan's interest rate changes.

- In the Preview Payment window, the principal and interest amount applies to the next scheduled payment only. That's because Quicken calculates the correct amounts of these numbers every time that you make a payment.

- You can specify whether you want to pay your loan with a handwritten check, an online banking transaction, or a printed check by selecting the appropriate radio button in the Preview Payment window.

Wells Fargo Payment Schedule				
Date	Pmt	Principal	Interest	Balance
			8.250%	21,575.98
9/15/98	1	230.32	148.33	21,345.66
10/15/98	2	231.90	146.75	21,113.76
11/15/98	3	233.49	145.16	20,880.27
12/15/98	4	235.10	143.55	20,645.17
1/15/99	5	236.71	141.94	20,408.46
2/15/99	6	238.34	140.31	20,170.12
3/15/99	7	239.98	138.67	19,930.14
4/15/99	8	241.63	137.02	19,688.51
5/15/99	9	243.29	135.36	19,445.22
6/15/99	10	244.96	133.69	19,200.26
7/15/99	11	246.65	132.00	18,953.61
8/15/99	12	248.34	130.31	18,705.27
9/15/99	13	250.05	128.60	18,455.22
10/15/99	14	251.77	126.88	18,203.45
11/15/99	15	253.50	125.15	17,949.95
12/15/99	16	255.24	123.41	17,694.71
1/15/00	17	257.00	121.65	17,437.71

Figure 14.7 You can review the payment schedule for any loan clicking the Payment Schedule button in the Loans window.

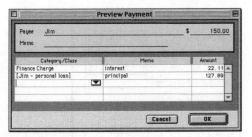

Figure 14.8 When you're the lender, the Preview Payment window is much simpler.

To create a loan (when you're lending):

1. Click the Loans button in the tool bar. The Loans window appears.

2. Click the New button. The Loan Interview window appears.

3. Select the Lending radio button and any others that are appropriate for this loan and then click the Continue button.

4. Fill out the information in the Set Up Loan window.

5. Click the Preview Payment button. As you can see in **Figure 14.8**, the Preview Payment window is small and uncomplicated when you're the lender.

CREATING LOANS

Making Loan Payments

To make a loan payment, you first recall the loan payment from the Loans list and enter it in the register of the bank account from which you're making the payment. Quicken then calculates the principal and interest amounts and updates the loan balance.

Of course, you don't have to do this manually if you have a fixed-rate loan. It's easy to schedule the loan payment for automatic entry using the Calendar (as discussed in Chapter 7).

To make a loan payment:

1. Open the account register or the Write Checks window for the bank account from which you'll make the loan payment.

2. Choose Edit > New Transaction, or press ⌘N.

3. Choose Lists > Loans. The Loans window appears.

4. Select the loan for which you want to enter a payment and click the Use button, or simply double-click on the loan.

   The Payment window appears (**Figure 14.9**).

5. If you need to make any adjustments in the Payment window, enter them now. For example, if you have a variable-rate interest loan, you should enter the current interest rate. You can also enter a prepayment if you want to pay off the loan faster.

6. Click the OK button.

   Quicken will enter the loan payment in the account register.

Figure 14.9 You can change the interest rate or add prepayment information in the loan Payment window.

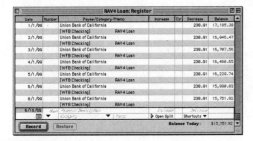

Figure 14.10 You can view the history of your loan at any time by opening the account register for the loan from the Accounts list.

✔ Tips

- To see the history of a loan, open the account register for the loan from the Accounts list. Your register should resemble the one shown in **Figure 14.10**.

- Loan payments are entered as split transactions. Open the split to see what portion went toward interest and what went to pay down the principal.

SETTING UP INVESTMENT ACCOUNTS

"Investing? Who needs it? Why, I'm only [fill in some number under 30] years old; I won't need to worry about retirement for a long time."

Sound familiar? When you're in your teens or twenties, retirement is a lifetime away. Ironically, that is just the time that you should begin investing, because you'll have nearly 50 years of compound interest working for you. Professional financial planners like to show how if you save just $100 per month starting when you're 20, you can easily retire with more than a million dollars. But if you wait until you're 30 and make the same investments, you end up with only about a third as much when you're 65.

(If you're already past your twenties and thirties, don't despair—it's never too late to start preparing for your future.)

For the vast majority of us, the key to comfortable living in future years and a successful retirement is a solid and consistent savings and investment program. Quicken lets you update current market values and see whether you're earning or losing money on your investments.

In this chapter, you'll learn how to set up and add to an investment portfolio and how to set up a mutual fund account in Quicken. So don't wait; get started on saving for the future today.

Using Investment Accounts

You can use a variety of account types within Quicken to track your investments (see **Table 15.1**). Here are the four choices:

◆ Use a regular bank account for investments with a constant share price or no share price. For example, a certificate of deposit (CD) earns interest, but because the interest rate is fixed when you buy the CD, the value doesn't go up or down according to a fluctuating market.

◆ Asset accounts are used to keep track of things that you own, such as personal property, real estate, or other tangible items. For example, if you have a valuable stamp or wine collection, you might track its value in an Asset account so that the collection shows up as part of your net worth. You can reassess and update the value of the collection in the Asset account from time to time.

◆ A portfolio account tracks one or more securities. (A security is an investment vehicle, such as a stock, bond, mutual fund, money-market fund, certificate of deposit, precious metal, or collectible.) Your portfolio account can include a mix of securities, and you can use the account to track transactions and provide the total market value for your portfolio. A good way of using portfolio accounts is to use one for each broker or other financial institution you use to handle a group of investments. Quicken's many reporting options can show you how your portfolio is performing.

◆ Each mutual fund account tracks a mutual fund. It's easier to use than the portfolio account if all you want to do is track a single mutual fund. (Of course, you can have as many mutual fund accounts as you wish, each tracking a different mutual fund.)

✔ **Tip**

■ One drawback of using a bank account or an asset account is that it cannot track the rate of return on an investment. To track a return rate, you'll need to use a portfolio or mutual fund account.

Table 15.1 If you're not sure which kind of account to use for your investments, take a look at Table 15.1 to see Intuit's recommendations.

Selecting the proper account type for your investment

Investment Type	Account Type
Securities for which you want to track a cash balance, such as stocks, bonds, or mutual funds; or a collection of investments in a brokerage account	Portfolio
A single mutual fund with no cash balance	Mutual fund
Money market funds	Bank (if you write checks against the fund) or mutual fund (if you need to track the rate of return)
Certificates of deposit	Bank
Real estate	Asset
IRA accounts, Keogh accounts, variable annuities Unit trusts Real estate investment trusts or partnerships	Portfolio
Treasury bills Fixed annuities, 401(k), 403 (b), pensions Collectibles or precious metals	Portfolio or asset

Setting up Your Portfolio

Before you get started setting up your portfolio accounts, you need to decide how much investment history you want to include in your records. You have three options: a complete history, just this year's information, or what I call the "Aw-the-heck-with-it" method—just enter your current investment holdings. (For a detailed rundown of the pros and cons of each method, see the Quicken User Guide.)

If you choose the complete history option, you'll need to enter the initial purchase price for each security and all subsequent transactions. On the plus side, all your reports are complete, and Quicken can accurately calculate capital gains. On the minus side, if you been investing for several years, that's a lot of data to enter. However, Intuit recommends this option, and so do I.

If you decide to enter just this year's data, you'll enter the investment balances as of the end of last year and then enter all of the transactions for each security since the beginning of this year. With this method, the information you need to find and enter is more recent and probably easier for you to obtain. Reports that deal with events from this year will be accurate, and if you sell a security, Quicken will be able to track which lots of that security you should sell to minimize or maximize your short-term capital gains. This method's disadvantage is that Quicken will not know the original cost of the security (called the *cost basis*), so you can't get accurate long-term capital gains or realized gain reports.

Figure 15.1 Click the Accounts button to set up a new account.

Figure 15.2 You can create a new portfolio from the Set Up Account window.

Figure 15.3 When you set up a new portfolio account, Quicken opens an associated account register.

The "Aw-the-heck-with-it" method is the fastest, and reports that cover events after today will be accurate. You just enter in your current investment holdings. On the other hand, data for this year and past years will be incomplete, and you won't be able to get reports for capital gains or realized gains. This is a significant drawback, so think twice before you decide to use this method.

To create a portfolio account:

1. Click the Accounts button in the tool bar or select Lists > Accounts to open the Accounts list (**Figure 15.1**). Click New. The Set Up Account window appears (**Figure 15.2**).

2. Select the Portfolio radio button.

3. Enter the name of the portfolio account in the Account Name box.

4. In the Description box, add a short description of the account (optional).

5. If the account is taxable, make sure that the Taxable box is checked. If this account is going to be tax-free, clear the Taxable box.

6. Click the Create button.

   Quicken opens a new account register for the new portfolio account (**Figure 15.3**).

To add securities to your portfolio:

1. Click the Portfolio button at the bottom of the new account register. The Portfolio window will appear (**Figure 15.4**), containing the account you just created.

   If you had previously created other investment accounts, they would appear in the Portfolio window as well. All investment accounts are listed in a single Portfolio window.

2. Click the Add Security button at the bottom of the Portfolio window.

   The Security Name dialog box appears (**Figure 15.5**).

3. Type in a name for the new security, and then click the OK button.

4. Quicken pops up a dialog box that says it can't find that security (**Figure 15.6**). Click the Set Up button.

   The Set Up Security window appears (**Figure 15.7**).

5. In the Symbol box, enter the stock ticker symbol for the security.

6. In the Type box, choose one of the options from the pop-up menu (Bond, CD, Mutual fund, or Stock).

7. In the Goal box, choose one of the options from the pop-up menu (College fund, Growth, High-risk, Income, or Low-risk).

8. Ignore the "Notify if price is" boxes.

Figure 15.4 The Portfolio window shows all of your investment accounts.

Figure 15.5 To add a security to your portfolio, enter its name.

Figure 15.6 Click the Set Up button to reassure Quicken that you want to create a new security.

Figure 15.7 Use the Set Up Security window to enter details of the new security.

Figure 15.8 Select an option from the Add Security dialog to tell Quicken that you own the security or that you're just keeping an eye on it.

Figure 15.9 You must indicate that you acquired the security before you began using Quicken or that you'll be transferring funds from another Quicken account to purchase the security.

9. If the security is taxable, make sure the "Taxable" box is checked. Make sure that the "Hide in lists" box is not checked.

10. Click the Create button.

    The Add Security dialog appears (**Figure 15.8**).

11. If you own the security, select the "Add shares to account" radio button and click OK. The Action Type List window appears.

    or

    If you don't own the security but want to track its performance, select "Add security to WatchList." Then click OK.

    You can add securities that interest you but that you don't yet own in the WatchList area to track how they do. If you choose this option, setup for that security is complete.

12. If you selected the "Add shares to account" radio button in step 11, the Action Type dialog box (**Figure 15.9**) appears. You must tell Quicken whether you acquired the security before or after you started using Quicken. Select "Move shares in" to add shares that you already owned to the portfolio account without using funds from any Quicken account to purchase those shares. Click OK and the Move Shares In window appears.

    or

    Select the "Buy" radio button to purchase shares with funds from another Quicken account. Click the OK button to open the Buy dialog box, and then go to step 15.

    (continued)

13. In the Move Shares In window, enter the date, the number of shares in the security that you own, the price you bought the shares for, and a memo (optional).

14. Click the Record button. The security shows up in the Portfolio window

15. If you selected "Buy" in step 12, the Buy dialog box appears (**Figure 15.10**). Fill in the date, the number of shares, the price you bought the shares for, the broker commission (if any), and the source of funds (must be another Quicken account). Click the Record button and the security will show up in the Portfolio window.

✔ Tips

- If you leave the Source of Funds field blank when purchasing a security, Quicken deducts the money for it from the Portfolio account.

- If you leave the Destination of Funds field blank when selling a security, Quicken credits the proceeds of the sale to the Portfolio account.

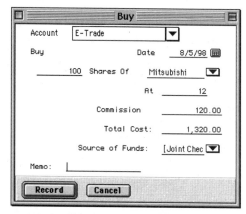

Figure 15.10 When you buy stocks, you always want to keep track of the purchase price and commission so that later, when you sell them, you can gauge your profit (or loss). Here you also note the source of funds with which you bought your shares.

Figure 15.11 Quicken maintains an account register for mutual funds, as with every other kind of account.

To add a mutual fund to your portfolio:

1. Click the Accounts button in the tool bar, or select Lists > Accounts from the menu, to open the Accounts list. Click New.

   The Set Up Account window appears (as shown in **Figure 15.2**).

2. Select the Mutual Fund radio button.

3. Enter the name of the mutual fund in the Account Name box.

4. In the Description box, add a short description of the mutual fund (optional).

5. If the mutual fund is taxable, make sure that the "Taxable" box is checked. If this is a tax-free fund, clear the "Taxable" box.

6. Click the Create button.

   Quicken opens an account register for the new mutual fund (**Figure 15.11**).

MANAGING YOUR INVESTMENTS

After setting up your investment portfolio (see Chapter 15), you need to manage your investments on an ongoing basis. That means updating the share prices of your securities and making entries whenever you buy or sell an investment.

Getting up-to-date quotes on stocks, bonds, and mutual funds is easy if you have access to the Internet. If you have a modem and access to the Internet, Quicken can download securities prices and enter them directly into your Portfolio window.

New to Quicken 2000 is the ability to download historical prices for securities.

Quicken also allows you to view and manually enter security prices in either the Portfolio window or the Security Detail window.

To manually update prices in the Portfolio window:

1. Click the Portfolio button in the tool bar (**Figure 16.1**) to open the Portfolio window (**Figure 16.2**).

2. At the top of the Portfolio window, you'll see a date next to "Set Prices As Of." If you're updating securities prices as of another day (the default is today's date), change this date.

3. Select a security in the Portfolio window by clicking on it, and then enter a share price for the displayed date by clicking at the appropriate spot in the Price column, as shown in **Figure 16.2**. You can enter a price either as a decimal number or as a fraction.

4. Click the Record button (or press the (Return) or (Enter) key) to save the new price. Quicken will recalculate the value of that security and your whole portfolio.

✔ Tips

■ In the Price column, you can increase or decrease the price by $1/8$ share (0.125) by pressing the plus ((+)) or hyphen ((-)) key.

■ If the prices in the Portfolio window appear to be incorrect, press (⌘)(Option)(U) to force a recalculation of your entire Portfolio.

Figure 16.1 Click the Portfolio button to open the Portfolio window.

Figure 16.2 You can use the Portfolio window to view all of your investments.

MANAGING YOUR INVESTMENTS

Figure 16.3 The Security Detail window provides a wealth of information about a security.

Figure 16.4 You can view the price history of the security from the Prices tab of the Security Detail window.

Figure 16.5 You can change a stock price in the New Price dialog.

To manually update prices in the Security Detail window:

1. In the Portfolio window, double-click on a security name, or click the Detail button at the bottom of the window. A Security Detail window will appear (**Figure 16.3**).

2. Click on the Prices tab (**Figure 16.4**).

3. Make necessary changes to the prices:

   ◆ To enter a new price, click the New button and fill out the New Price dialog (**Figure 16.5**); then click the Record button.

   ◆ To change a price, click the Edit button, fill out the Edit Price dialog (which looks almost identical to the New Price dialog), and then click the Change button.

   ◆ To delete a price, select the price that you wish to delete and click the Delete button. Quicken will ask you to confirm the deletion. Choose OK to confirm.

To download price quotes:

1. Click the Quotes button in the tool bar (**Figure 16.6**).

   Quicken will connect to the online service you specified in Preferences and download the latest prices of your securities.

2. The Download Summary window (**Figure 16.7**) opens, showing how many quotes were downloaded and when. Click "View Latest Prices."

   A Quicken Quotes window shows you the downloaded price information for every security in your Portfolio (**Figure 16.8**). At the same time, your portfolio is automatically updated.

✔ Tips

- You can download prices as many times per day you wish, but Quicken stores only one price per day. Every time you click the Store Current Prices button, Quicken replaces the prices in your Portfolio with the most recent price.

- The stock symbols in your setup must be exactly the same as those used by the markets. If the message "Ticker not found" appears in your Quicken Quotes window, check to make sure that your stock symbols are correct.

- Stocks, options, and indexes are updated constantly during the business day, although the quotes you get online are delayed by about 20 minutes. Prices for mutual funds are updated only once per day at 6 p.m. Eastern time.

Figure 16.6 Click the Quotes button to download security quotes.

Figure 16.7 The Download Summary window opens when the quotes have been downloaded.

Symbol	Volume	High	Low	Current	Change	Time/Date
ADBE	0	.000	.000	39.938	unchanged	7/20/98
AAPL	0	.000	.000	36.875	unchanged	7/20/98
BSPT	0	.000	.000	9.938	unchanged	7/20/98
CML	0	.000	.000	1.125	unchanged	7/20/98
CPQ	0	.000	.000	33.938	unchanged	7/20/98
FGRIX	0	.000	.000	46.210	unchanged	7/20/98
FMAGX	0	.000	.000	115.950	unchanged	7/20/98
F	0	.000	.000	58.875	unchanged	7/20/98
GM	0	.000	.000	69.875	unchanged	7/20/98
IBM	0	.000	.000	120.188	unchanged	7/20/98
INTU	0	.000	.000	64.125	unchanged	7/20/98

All quotes are at least 15 minutes delayed

Store Current Prices

Figure 16.8 The Quicken Quotes window shows the downloaded information for your portfolio.

MANAGING YOUR INVESTMENTS

Figure 16.9 Click the Historical Price button on the tool bar.

Figure 16.10 The Download Historical Prices dialog box opens.

Using Quicken.com's Investment Tools

In the Investment area, Quicken.com offers a broad spectrum of tools that should prove very useful to the investor. Many of these features are discussed in Chapter 19.

One of Quicken's strengths is its integration with the Internet. As working online has become more and more the norm, Intuit has shifted many of its functions to the Internet, which keeps the product up to date with current market trends and changing technologies.

Quicken allows you to download not only today's prices from the Quicken.com server, but up to five years of historical information for both stocks and mutual funds as well. This is an invaluable tool for making decisions about your investment strategies.

To download historical prices:

1. Choose Online > Historical Prices, or click the Historical Price button (**Figure 16.9**) on the tool bar.

   The Download Historical Prices dialog box opens (**Figure 16.10**).

2. Choose the securities you want to research from the list of stocks in your portfolio, and select the time period for which you want quotes. Then click Download.

   Quicken logs onto the Internet and downloads the information you specified and adds it to your portfolio data.

3. To view the information, open the Security Detail window, as described previously.

USING QUICKEN.COM'S INVESTMENT TOOLS

Buying and Selling Securities

Most of the transactions in your investment accounts will involve buying or selling securities, but Quicken can handle virtually any sort of investment transaction. **Table 16.1** shows the transactions available in Quicken. The investment process is so complex that I don't have room to explain it all here. Refer to the Quicken User Manual to learn about complex investment transactions.

You can enter investment transactions by two methods: by using investment forms or by entering information directly into the investment account register. The investment forms are easier to use, especially if you're new to these sorts of transactions. After you become familiar with investment transactions, you may choose to use the other entry method, which is to simply enter the information into the investment account register.

Table 16.1

Investment actions	
ACTION	DESCRIPTION
Buy	Buy security with cash
Capital Gain Long	Receive cash from long-term capital gains distribution
Capital Gain Short	Receive cash from short-term capital gains distribution
Dividend	Receive cash from dividend
Interest Income	Receive cash from interest income
Miscellaneous Expense	Pay miscellaneous expense with cash
Miscellaneous Income	Receive cash from miscellaneous income
Move Shares In	Add shares to account
Move Shares Out	Remove shares from account
Reinvest Dividend	Reinvest in shares of the security with money from dividend or income distribution
Reinvest Interest	Reinvest in shares of the security with money from interest distribution
Reinvest Long	Reinvest in shares of the security with money from long-term capital gains distribution
Reinvest Short	Reinvest in shares of the security with money from short-term capital gains distribution
Return of Capital	Receive cash from return of capital
Sell	Sell security and receive cash
Stock Split	Change number of shares as result of stock split
Transfer Money	Transfer money into or out of this account

Figure 16.11 Begin an investment transaction by clicking the Actions button in the tool bar.

Figure 16.12 Choose the kind of investment transaction you want in the Investment Actions window.

Figure 16.13 Fill out the investment detail window to complete your transaction.

To use investment forms for transactions:

1. Click the Portfolio button in the tool bar to open the Portfolio window.

2. Click on a security to select it in the Portfolio window.

3. Click the Actions button in the tool bar (**Figure 16.11**).

   The Investment Actions window appears (**Figure 16.12**).

4. Find the transaction that you wish to perform in the Investment Actions window, and double-click it.

   The detail window for the transaction you choose opens (**Figure 16.13**). (In this case, Sell was chosen in the Investment Actions window.)

5. Fill out the information in the detail window, and then click the Record button.

✔ Tip

■ If you're selling a security, you might want to choose which shares to sell, so that you get the most favorable capital gains treatment. In the detail window, click the Choose Lots button to pick a particular batch of shares to sell.

Planning for the Future

One of the things I like about Quicken is its ability to shed light on the past, present, and future of my financial life. I can use it to look back to where I've been, to deal with my current finances, and to help me create my future financial scenario.

Sometimes I just want to look a little way into the future, so I use the Financial Calendar to see which payments are scheduled for next month. If my finances were a bit more predictable (that they aren't is a side effect of my life as a freelance writer), I might be interested in creating a yearly budget. However, I do plan to retire someday, so I use Quicken's retirement planners to see whether I'm on track with my savings and investment programs.

Quicken Deluxe 2000 includes two tools under the Financial Fitness banner that can help you now as well as in the future: the Emergency Records Organizer and the Tax Deduction Finder. In addition, Quicken Home Inventory is a small free-standing application that lets you go through your house room by room from the basement to the attic to make an exhaustive inventory of your possessions and their monetary values for insurance purposes.

Through Quicken's connections to the
Quicken.com Web site, you are a button's
push away from the Retirement Planner and
the Life Event Planner to help you make sure
your resources will be sufficient when the
time comes for your kids' college tuition, or
the trip of your lifetime, or that wedding
they'll be talking about for years. In a similar
vein, Quicken.com gives access to your credit
report and to a Debt Reduction Planner
that will guide you through the process of
paying down your debt as efficiently as possible, potentially saving you a lot of money
that might otherwise go to the finance company as interest.

In this chapter you'll learn how to use the
Financial Fitness planners and some of
Quicken's other tools that can help you take
control of your finances now and plan for
your future financial well-being.

Using the Financial Fitness Tools

Quicken Deluxe 2000 includes three programs in the Activities menu. The two under the Financial Fitness heading walk you through the process of collecting the relevant information, such as the locations of all your important documents and a list of tax deductions for which you may be eligible; Quicken Home Inventory helps you create an exhaustive list of your possessions and their values.

To make your work easier, these planners include audio and QuickTime movies that show examples and illustrate financial concepts. To hear the sounds and view the movies, the Quicken Deluxe CD must be in your CD-ROM drive. You can also run the Financial Fitness programs without the CD (but you'll miss the multimedia treats).

Financial Fitness Limitations

Although the Financial Fitness tools give you valuable information and viable action plans, you shouldn't rely on them as your sole source for financial planning.

The reason for this is simple: The world has changed in the time since these programs were written. Intuit did not update some of these programs from their previous versions that shipped with Quicken 98. For example, the Tax Deduction Finder is based on 1997 tax year information and the tax law has changed since then. Other programs, such as the Retirement Planner, contain assumptions that could no longer be completely accurate or don't take into account new financial instruments that can provide significant savings for some people.

The Financial Fitness planners are good guides, but don't take them as gospel. And before you make any big financial moves, it's always a good idea to consult your accountant or financial planner.

Here's a rundown of Quicken's three Financial Fitness tools:

 The **Emergency Records Organizer** helps you gather and track important financial and legal documents. It produces a variety of customized reports as well as a Comprehensive Report containing all the information you enter, and an Emergency Report with important contact numbers, medical, and health insurance information.

 The less tax you pay, the better your bottom line. By taking you through the survey step by step with a set of questions about each of a long list of possible deductions, the **Tax Deduction Finder** helps you determine whether you're eligible for certain tax deductions.

 The **Quicken Home Inventory** program helps jog your memory about all the valuable things you own and even goes so far as to suggest replacement and resale values for these items. It includes information on your various insurance policies and helps you determine whether you have adequate coverage.

Web-Based Planners

You get to Quicken's Web-based planners by choosing them from the hierarchical menu that you see after you choose Online > To the Web. They can also be reached by clicking their buttons on the tool bar. These planners can help you go beyond the bookkeeping functions Quicken provides to take a more active role in the direction of your financial existence.

Each Web-based planner displays a menu on the left side of the screen that shows the topics covered by the planner. You can jump to any topic by clicking it, but it's usually best to work through the planner sequentially.

In the main part of the planner window, you'll see a worksheet, where you answer questions about your finances. At the end of the process, Quicken will show you an action plan—the actual steps you need to take to achieve your stated goal—that you can print out and use.

 The **Retirement Planner** probes your savings and investment plans and tells you whether your current plan (if you have one) is adequate to meet your needs when you retire. If it's not, the planner will come up with a new plan to help you meet your goals.

 The **Life Events Planners** are similar to the Retirement Planner; they measure your projected earnings, investments, and savings against some major future expense you want to plan for. Quicken lists college, weddings, and parenting, but obviously you can choose other kinds of goals as well. If Quicken determines that you can't afford the expense(s), the planners offer some suggestions to help you create a successful financial plan that will enable you to meet expenses.

Many people are carrying too large a load of consumer debt, and the **Debt Reduction Planner** will show you how to get out of debt faster and save money while doing it. If you follow the recommendations in this planner, you can save hundreds or even thousands of dollars in interest payments.

The final Financial Fitness tool is a **Free Credit Report** that you can request from one of the major credit reporting agencies. The report will be delivered to your home address within four to six weeks. You can opt to pay a fee for faster delivery, or pay a larger fee to get a consolidated report from all three of the major US credit bureaus.

Because each planner is used in a similar way, I'll go into only two of them in detail here: the Retirement Planner and the Debt Reduction Planner.

WEB-BASED PLANNERS

✔ Tip

- It's a good idea to take advantage of the Free Credit Report, or the more expensive, extra-value credit reports. It's an especially good idea to see your credit report before you purchase a major-ticket item like a house or a car. You want to have the same information that the mortgage or finance company will use when they decide how credit-worthy you are. Because I'm buying a house, I recently paid for the consolidated bureau report, and it was interesting reading. It led me to contact one of the credit bureaus to remove inaccurate information; they had my occupation listed as "school bus driver," which was a job I had more than 20 years ago when I was a college student! What I learned was that once data gets into the credit bureau computers, it may never come out. Best to get a report every few years just to check for inaccuracies. If you've been turned down for credit based on the information in a credit report, by federal law you are entitled to a free copy of your report from the credit bureau that supplied the report.

The Retirement Planner

Careful planning can make your retirement years much more enjoyable and can significantly reduce anxiety levels in the years preceding them. Matching your earning levels to your investments and making realistic decisions about what kind of expenses you will have in the future are the keys to successful retirement planning. Quicken's Retirement Planner is one way of balancing your current needs against your future ones and optimizing the overall picture.

To set up a Retirement Plan:

1. Click the Retirement Planner button on the tool bar (**Figure 17.1**) or choose Online > To the Web > Retirement Planner.

   Quicken will open the browser you selected (back in Chapter 11) in the Preferences window and go to the Retirement Planner on the Quicken Web site.

2. After reading over the introductory material on the Retirement Planner page, click the "Build your plan now" button to open the Personal Information worksheet (**Figure 17.2**). Fill in the required data and then click Next.

3. In the Salary worksheet (**Figure 17.3**), enter your salary and that of your spouse (if you are in this thing together). Guesstimate your annual increases and your future cost of living, and then click Next.

Figure 17.1 The Retirement Planner button on the tool bar launches your browser and directs you to the Quicken.com Web site.

Figure 17.2 Enter your personal information and click Next to go on.

Figure 17.3 Enter salary information in this window.

Figure 17.4 The economic assumptions you make have a lot to do with the ultimate success of your plan.

Figure 17.5 Fill in information about your current and predicted assets.

Figure 17.6 Here is where you enter information about your social security and pension benefits.

4. In the Economic Assumptions worksheet (**Figure 17.4**), you can let Quicken estimate your tax rate and project a rate of inflation or you can use your own, perhaps more conservative, figures. Then click Next.

5. The Assets worksheet (**Figure 17.5**) asks about your current investments and how they are growing. Fill in the blanks and click Next.

6. The Retirement Benefits worksheet (**Figure 17.6**) sets up the assumptions about what your income will be after retirement. Click Next.

(continued)

THE RETIREMENT PLANNER

7. In the Risk & Return (**Figure 17.7**) work-sheet, you can set goals for the rate of return on your investments. Click Next.

8. The Results window (**Figure 17.8**) shows a graph of your portfolio value. Using the pop-up, you can also view income, savings, or expenses. If you plan is succeeding, you'll see a green light; if not, you'll see a red light; if you might be in trouble, you'll see a yellow light.

9. Scrolling down, you come to the What-If section (**Figure 17.9**) that makes the retirement planning process so useful. You can change the variables and see what happens, from wildly optimistic assumptions, to financial Armageddon. Change a number and click the Recalculate button to get the new result. The Solve button next to each box asks Quicken to figure out what that number needs to be to make the plan work. Click Next to go to the final screen.

Figure 17.7 The Risk & Return window shows a way of diversifying your portfolio to meet your goal.

Figure 17.8 The results are shown here in graphic fashion. If your plan succeeds, you'll get the green light. Otherwise, go back and make some changes.

Figure 17.9 The What-If section allows you to play with the numbers.

THE RETIREMENT PLANNER

1. Save according to your saving schedule
Consider setting up an automatic savings plan for the following amounts:

Savings Schedule 1999

Savings	Monthly	Yearly
Taxable	$0	$0
Your tax-deferred*	$500	$6,000
Spouse tax-deferred*	$375	$4,500
Total Savings	$875	$10,500

*Includes employer matches, if any

2. Allocate your savings
Consider setting up an automatic investment plan with your bank, brokerage firm, or mutual fund company. If you want to use the investment mix suggested by Callan Associates, invest your savings in the following asset classes:

Suggested Investment Schedule 1999

Overall Portfolio (10.0% Return)		Monthly	Yearly
Domestic Bonds	24.0%	$210	$2,520
Large Cap Stocks	41.0%	$359	$4,305
Small Cap Stocks	9.0%	$79	$945
International Stocks	26.0%	$227	$2,730
Total Overall Portfolio		$875	$10,500

Next steps

- Help me find mutual funds to invest in for my retirement
- Help me find individual stocks to invest in for my retirement

Figure 17.10 Here is the Action Plan you'll need to follow to make your retirement a comfortable one.

10. The last window of the series (**Figure 17.10**) is the Action Plan.

At the top of the window is the plan summary that contains all the information you entered as you went along. At the bottom are a Savings Schedule and a Suggested Investment Schedule that shows a way for you to allocate your investments. If you stick to the plan, you have reasonable assurance of achieving your goal. This is the proverbial bottom line.

Reducing Consumer Debt

Paying off your credit card and loan debts is an important step toward financial happiness. If you don't pay off your credit card and loan bills in full every month, you are charged interest to compensate the bank for your use of their money. Unfortunately, interest payments aren't a good deal for you; the money that you pay in interest is unproductive and could be spent in better ways.

Quicken's Debt Reduction Planner uses a simple philosophy. It analyzes your debt and pays off the highest interest rate cards first, which lets you get out of debt faster while paying less interest.

To use the Debt Reduction Planner:

1. Click the Debt Plan button on the task bar (**Figure 17.11**).

   The Debt Reduction Planner Introduction window appears (**Figure 17.12**).

2. If you want to read one of the topics listed under "Overview," click on it. Then click Next.

3. The Debts window appears (**Figure 17.13**). Enter the information for each debt and then click Save to add it to the "Your debts" list at the right. Click New to enter a new debt. When you're done, click Next to go on to the Summary window.

Figure 17.11 Click the Debt Plan button to go to the Debt Reduction Planner on the Web site.

Figure 17.12 You can ask questions about reducing your debt in the Introduction window.

Figure 17.13 The Debts window is where you begin the process by listing what you owe and to whom.

REDUCING CONSUMER DEBT

Figure 17.14 The Summary window adds it all up and tells the sad story.

Figure 17.15 The Payment window shows how you can improve your situation by simply restructuring you payments.

Figure 17.16 If you can use some of your savings to pay off part of your debt, you may find your situation seems much rosier.

4. The Summary window (**Figure 17.14**) shows what you owe, what your monthly payments are, when you'll be debt free, and what the total interest paid will be. When you're over the shock, click Next.

5. In the Payment window (**Figure 17.15**), Quicken begins to show how you can save some money and get out of debt sooner. Simply following the plan outlined on this page will help considerably. To do even better, click Next.

6. The Savings window (**Figure 17.16**) counsels you to apply some of your savings to pay down your debt immediately. Pick a figure you think you can afford and type it into the text field. Then click Save/Recalculate to see how much you can save and how soon you will be free of debt. When you have reached a figure you're comfortable with, click Next.

(continued)

7. In the Expenses window (**Figure 17.17**), you'll cut back on your expenditures and use the money to retire your debt. This window demonstrates immediately how this will benefit you. Set a figure, see how much it improves the results of your debt reduction plan, and click Next.

8. The Results window (**Figure 17.18**) is a very impressive argument for keeping to the plan you have developed in the previous steps. Meditate on it and then click Next.

Figure 17.17 Cutting back on your spending and using the money to pay off your creditors can help as well.

Figure 17.18 The Results window presents a convincing argument for following the plan's recommendations.

Spending Savings to Reduce Debt

If you already have some money saved, you might question the wisdom of taking money out of your savings or investment accounts to help pay off your consumer debt. Although it is a smart idea to have a financial cushion, you need to ask yourself if your money is working for you in the best way.

For example, assume that you have $2,000 in an investment that is earning 10 percent interest, but your credit cards are charging you 16 percent interest. At the end of the year, you'll have lost money by not paying off your credit cards. You're better off reducing your debt as quickly as possible.

Figure 17.19 The action plan makes it all very concrete.

Figure 17.20 Here is the schedule of payments you need to make.

Figure 17.21 This window offers other resources you may want to check into.

9. Across the top of the Action Plan window (**Figure 17.19**), you'll see the steps you need to take to follow the plan you have written. Below that is a schedule of your payments to your lenders (**Figure 17.20**) that optimizes your debt reduction.

10. The final window, Next Steps (**Figure 17.21**), refers you to other resources available to you that can help get you out of debt.

✔ Tip

■ It's often more useful to leave your home and auto loans out of the Debt Reduction Planner, because these represent assets as well as liabilities. What you should focus on in debt reduction is expensive consumer debt such as credit cards.

REDUCING CONSUMER DEBT

Getting Organized

So many documents in our lives are important, yet most of us don't bother to keep them in one place, ready for easy access in the event that a family member or we will need them.

The **Emergency Records Organizer** helps you bring together all of the information that you, your family, or your friends would need in an emergency, such as medical insurance information, medical contacts, bank accounts, and even wills and other legal documents.

Because each section in the Emergency Records Organizer works in a similar fashion, I'm going to discuss the planner's highlights rather than take you through every possible step.

To use the Emergency Records Organizer:

1. Choose Activities > Financial Fitness > Emergency Records Organizer. The Organizer's Getting Started window appears (**Figure 17.22**). Click Next to begin.

2. Click on a question to view a QuickTime movie about that question. When you're done asking questions, click the Next button to open the Security window (**Figure 17.23**).

3. If you want to protect your emergency records file from prying eyes, enter a password, and then enter it again for verification. Click Next to open the Personal Information window (**Figure 17.24**).

Figure 17.22 You can ask Quicken these questions before you get started.

Figure 17.23 To protect your essential information from others who may be using your computer, type in a password.

Figure 17.24 Enter your name, address, telephone number, and other personal information here.

GETTING ORGANIZED

Figure 17.25 Fill in additional personal information in this window.

Figure 17.26 Indicate the type of contacts you want to enter.

Figure 17.27 After you indicate the contact category, enter each contact's name in this window.

4. Fill in your name, address, telephone number, date of birth, and Social Security number. Then click the "Add more info" button.

The More Personal Information window appears (**Figure 17.25**).

5. Fill in your driver's license number, your mother's maiden name, and other ID information, such as the license numbers of any professional licenses you hold. Also include any vital medical warnings, such as allergies. Click OK to return to the Personal Information window.

6. Click the Next button to enter the "Contracts & legal records" area. Read the information explaining what's in this section, and then click the Next button to open the Who to Call window (**Figure 17.26**).

7. Under the Contacts heading, choose one of the contact categories. An entry screen will appear in the middle of the window (**Figure 17.27**), where you can type in information about your contacts.

(continued)

8. Fill in the information in the entry screen, and then click the New button if you want to add more people in that category. Click on another category of Contacts to add information to that category. When you're done adding contacts, click the Next button to get to the "Legal documents" area (**Figure 17.28**).

9. Choose one of the Document types to begin filling out a form describing that document. Repeat as necessary for all of the document types you wish to enter.

10. Repeat the entry steps above for all of the Financial Data and Possessions sections in which you want to enter data. When you're done, click "Print your records" from the checklist on the right side of the window.

The Print Your Records window appears (**Figure 17.29**).

11. Click an icon to choose what type of report you want to print:

◆ The Emergency Report prints contact numbers, medical history, and insurance information.

◆ The Comprehensive Report prints all of the information you entered.

◆ Click Choose a Section to pick the sections of the Organizer that you want to print.

A preview dialog box will open, showing you how the report will look when printed.

12. Click the Print button to print your report.

Figure 17.28 Organize and keep track of all your important documents in this window.

Figure 17.29 You can print three kinds of reports.

Figure 17.30 Use the financial planning calculators for quick "what-if?" analyses.

Using the Financial Calculators

Quicken Deluxe 2000 includes six financial planning calculators to let you try "what if?" scenarios. You can use these calculators to get quick answers when you're considering a financial move, such as taking on a new mortgage. Five of the financial planning calculators work in basically the same way— except that the information you enter and the calculations Quicken makes will be different. See Chapter 18 for information on using the sixth calculator, the Quicken Tax Planner.

To use a financial calculator:

1. Choose Activities > Planning Calculators, and then choose the calculator that you want from the six on the menu.

   The calculator screen opens (**Figure 17.30**).

2. Click the arrow next to the type of calculation that you want Quicken to figure out.

3. Enter information into the calculator, and Quicken displays the results.

QUICKEN AT TAX TIME

Personally, I don't know anyone who enjoys paying taxes. I've heard that such people actually exist, but I've never met them. For the rest of us, preparing and paying taxes is a yearly ritual that we could easily live without.

Quicken can help to ease some of the pain (although if you end up writing a check instead of receiving a refund, Quicken can't do anything about the agony you'll feel). By properly categorizing your income and expenses throughout the year, you'll be able to create reports that make filling out your tax forms much easier. Using these reports can also save you money if your taxes are prepared by someone else, because the preparer will have less digging to do to get a clear picture of your financial situation.

If you're the do-it-yourself type, you can export Quicken data to a tax preparation program called MacInTax, also made by Intuit. With federal and state tax forms built in, MacInTax can do a complete job of tax preparation, from finding information to calculating and printing your final tax return.

When it comes to taxes, I hate surprises. I use the Quicken Tax Planner to get a ballpark figure for my taxes before I see my accountant.

In this chapter, you'll see how to do some tax planning, create these reports, and get your Quicken data ready for MacInTax.

Planning for Taxes

You can't avoid paying taxes altogether, but it's perfectly OK to work hard at finding and using every tax deduction that you can legally claim. Quicken has two tools that you can use to help reduce for tax load: the Tax Deduction Finder, one of the Financial Fitness planners available in Quicken Deluxe 2000; and the Quicken Tax Planner, a financial calculator that lets you try out different tax scenarios.

To use the Tax Deduction Finder:

1. Insert the Quicken Deluxe 2000 CD in your CD-ROM drive so that you'll be able to experience the Tax Deduction Finder's QuickTime movies and audio help.

2. Choose Activities > Financial Fitness > Tax Deduction Finder. The Tax Deduction Finder's "Getting started" screen appears (**Figure 18.1**).

3. Play each of the three introductory QuickTime movies by clicking the square buttons next to the title of each movie. Then click the Next button. The "Personal info" screen appears (**Figure 18.2**).

4. Fill in the personal information requested in the screen. If you click "Yes" to the question "Are you married?" boxes will appear for you to enter your spouse's information. Click the Next button, and the Deductions introduction screen appears (**Figure 18.3**).

Figure 18.1 Click topics on the "Getting started" screen to watch and hear about Quicken's Tax Deduction Finder.

Figure 18.2 Enter information about you and your spouse in this screen.

Figure 18.3 Read this screen for information about deductions.

Figure 18.4 Choose a deduction category on the left and answer questions on the right to determine potential tax deductions.

Figure 18.5 Click OK to add a deduction category to your Quicken data file.

5. Read the information on the "Deduction" screen, and then click the Next button. The "Employee" screen appears (**Figure 18.4**).

6. The Tax Deduction Finder tests to determine whether you qualify for a particular deduction by asking you a series of questions about each deduction. Select a deduction from the scrolling list on the left side of the screen and, on the right side, click Yes or No to answer each question. The planner will tell you either that you can't take the deduction or that you may be eligible for the deduction.

   If you do possibly qualify for the deduction, the Create Quicken Category window (**Figure 18.5**) appears, asking if you wish to add a category covering the deduction to your Quicken data file. You can edit the name of the proposed category or add the category as listed. Then click the OK button. If you don't want to add the category, click the Cancel button.

7. Continue choosing deductions in the scrolling list on the left side of the screen until you have worked through all the deductions that you think may possibly apply to you. Then click the Next button to go to the next deduction screen ("Homeowner") or click one of the other types in the Deductions area to go directly to that screen.

(continued)

PLANNING FOR TAXES

8. When you have worked through all of the areas under Deductions, click Results in the menu on the right side of the screen. The "Results" introduction screen appears (**Figure 18.6**). Read the information, and then click the Next button. The "Summary" screen appears (**Figure 18.7**), listing your deduction categories.

9. Review the Summary screen, and then click the Next button. The "Action Plan" screen appears (**Figure 18.8**).

10. If you want a copy of your action plan to show to your tax preparer, click the Print button.

✔ Tip

■ The Tax Deduction Finder uses internal information based on the 1998 tax year. Since the tax code changes every year, you'll want to make sure that you check over the recommendations in your action plan with your accountant or with another tax professional. Or you can call the Internal Revenue Service with general tax questions at (800)829-1040.

Figure 18.6 Read the information in the Results screen to find out what happens next.

Figure 18.7 You can see a summary of your tax deductions on this screen.

Figure 18.8 Print a copy of your tax deduction action plan for your accountant from this screen.

PLANNING FOR TAXES

Figure 18.9 In the Quicken Tax Plan Window, click the "Use Quicken Info" button and Quicken will insert your pre-entered data.

To use the Tax Planner:

1. Choose Activities > Planning Calculators > Tax. The Quicken Tax Planner window appears (**Figure 18.9**).

2. Under "Filing Status and Tax Year" at the top of the window, choose your filing status and the tax year from the pop-up menus.

3. Click the "Use Quicken Info" button at the bottom of the window to have the planner import your financial data from the data file.

4. Click the "Tax Links" button at the bottom of the window to open the Assign Tax Links window, where you can assign Quicken categories to specific line items on federal tax forms.

For more information about Tax Links, see Chapter 3. (In general, the more Tax Links you assign the better, in terms of the Quicken Tax Planner's accuracy.)

5. You can click any of the buttons in the Income or Tax Computation areas to enter detailed information.

6. After you have entered all your tax information, the tax planner calculates your total tax, which shows you the amount you owe the IRS or the amount of your refund.

✔ Tip

■ If you want to see the tax implications of decisions such as buying a home, or filing taxes jointly or separately, you can try out three different tax scenarios and Quicken will give you the results. Click the Scenarios radio buttons, fill in the alternate information, and then switch between the tax scenarios to compare how each turns out.

PLANNING FOR TAXES

Creating Tax Reports

Your accountant will probably be interested in four kinds of Quicken reports while preparing your tax return:

- ◆ A **Category Summary** report shows the totals for all of your income and expense categories.

- ◆ A **Tax Summary** report shows your tax-related income and expenses, subtotaled by category.

- ◆ The **Tax Schedule** report groups information from all accounts in your data file that have tax lines assigned to them. The report lists information is grouped by tax form.

- ◆ A **Capital Gains** report shows the realized capital gains from your investment accounts.

You create and print each of these reports in almost exactly the same way. (For more information about creating reports, see Chapter 12.)

Figure 18.10 You can ask Quicken to create specific tax reports from this window.

Figure 18.11 This Tax Schedule report shows you the results of your Tax Links, organized by the federal forms to which they pertain.

To create a tax report:

1. Click the Reports button in the tool bar or choose Activities > Reports & Graphs > Reports to open the Reports window (**Figure 18.10**).

2. Click on the Standard tab in the Reports window, and then click Category Summary, Tax Schedule, or Tax Summary in the scrolling list on the left side of the window.

   or

   Click on the Investment tab in the Reports window, and then click Capital Gains in the scrolling list on the left side of the window.

3. Change the date range in the bottom of the window to print reports for particular dates, as needed.

4. Click the Create button. Quicken creates and displays the report (**Figure 18.11**).

CREATING TAX REPORTS

Exporting Quicken Data to MacInTax

Quicken can save data from a tax schedule report or a capital gains report in a format that's compatible with MacInTax. This format is called Tax Exchange Format (TXF). MacInTax can then read in the TXF file, saving you from having to do a lot of repetitive data entry.

To export Quicken data:

1. Create the tax report you want to export, and leave it open on your screen.

2. Choose File > Export Report. The standard Save dialog box will appear (**Figure 18.12**).

3. Enter a name for the report file in the "Export to File" box.

4. Click the MacInTax (TXF) button.

5. Click the Save button.

✔ Tip

■ If the MacInTax (TXF) button is not visible in the Save dialog box, it is probably because you have created a report that isn't a tax schedule or capital gains report and therefore isn't appropriate to send to MacInTax.

Figure 18.12 For the report to format properly for MacInTax, you must select the MacInTax (TXF) radio button in the Save dialog box.

USING QUICKEN.COM

Quicken is a terrific tool for helping you manage your money, but these days, an incredible amount of financial options are available to you. To make smart financial decisions, you're going to need up-to-date financial and investment information. That's where Quicken.com, Intuit's huge Web site at `http://www.quicken.com`, comes in.

Quicken.com offers up-to-the-minute news, price quotes, and information about the securities markets; tips from financial experts; access to online stock brokerages; retirement planning tools; and current tax information, including explanations of wacky changes Congress makes in the tax code.

The Web site tries to cover every aspect of your financial life by organizing its content into 10 departments: Investments, Home & Mortgage, Insurance, Taxes, Banking & Credit, Small Business, Retirement, Life Events, Saving & Spending, and Financial Forums. In this chapter, you'll see how to use some of Quicken.com's financial tools. Alas, I barely have room to scratch the surface. But do spend some time browsing the site; it will be time well spent.

Getting Around on Quicken.com

Before you start browsing the site, you should know what equipment and software you need to view Quicken.com. At a minimum, you'll need the following:

◆ A modem or another connection device. If you're using a modem (most people are), its speed should be at least 28.8 kilobits per second (Kbps). These days, most modems currently sold are 56 Kbps. If you're lucky enough to have a faster connection to the Internet, such as a cable modem, a DSL or ISDN line, or a local area network, so much the better.

◆ An account with an Internet Service Provider (ISP). An ISP sells access to the Internet. When you sign up with an ISP, you usually get an e-mail account and the ability to create your own Web site, as well as access to the various Internet services. Many people use America Online as their ISP.

◆ Web browsing software. Microsoft Internet Explorer 4.5 is included on the Quicken Deluxe 2000 CD-ROM.

The process of getting an account with an ISP and signing onto the Internet for the first time is beyond the scope of this book, so I will assume you've taken care of that part.

Figure 19.1 When you log on to Quicken.com, this page shows you the way to the site's helpful information.

For more on Quicken.com:

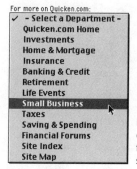

Figure 19.2 Choose one of the departments from this pop-up menu to find specific information.

To log on to Quicken.com:

1. Choose Online > To the Web > Quicken Home Page.

   You should see a screen like the one shown in **Figure 19.1**. If you get to Quicken.com and the screen looks different, chances are Intuit has redesigned the site since I wrote this book in the summer of 1999. Don't panic; companies are forever changing their Web sites. Just poke around until you find what you're looking for. Believe me, there is enough stuff here—if you were to follow all the links—to keep you entertained for days.

2. Along the left side of the screen, in the Departments navigation bar, you can click one of Quicken.com's department names to open that department's page.

   Financial news takes up the middle of the window, and a Mini Portfolio table appears on the right.

   or

   At the bottom of the browser window (not shown in Figure 19.1) is a navigation pop-up menu (**Figure 19.2**) that reveals the Quicken.com department names. Choose one of the departments from the pop-up menu to tell your browser to go to that department's page.

✔ Tips

- The navigation pop-up menu is available anywhere on the Quicken.com site, whereas the left navigation bar changes depending on which department you're in.

- If you need to return to a previous page, use the Back button at the top of the browser window.

- You can click the Quicken.com logo at the top of most pages on the site to return to the Quicken.com home page.

GETTING AROUND ON QUICKEN.COM

Finding Investment Information

The Quicken.com department people use most often is Investments. It's impossible to discuss everything you could do in the Investments department in the amount of space that I have here, so I'll focus on just a few common tasks.

To find a security quote:

1. If you're interested in a quote on a particular security, and you know the security's ticker symbol, type the symbol in the "Quotes and Research" area in the "Enter symbol" box.

2. Click the Go button, and a detailed quote page for the security appears (**Figure 19.3**).

3. If you're interested in finding out other information about the same security, choose an option from among the links that run down the left side of the page, under the security's name.

   (For example, after you click the Chart link, you'll see a page that looks like **Figure 19.4.**)

4. Continue your research on the stock by clicking other links from the left column or by modifying the type of chart or the period it covers from the pull-down menus that appear above it.

✔ Tip

- You can add another stock to the chart by typing its symbol into the Symbols box at the top of the page. Quicken will even help you find the stock's competitors with the "Stock Comparison" lookup feature that appears next to the box.

Figure 19.3 Type a stock's symbol in the box under "Quotes and Research" and then click the Go button to see information about a particular security.

Figure 19.4 Click the Chart link on the quotes page to see a chart showing information about the security.

FINDING INVESTMENT INFORMATION

Figure 19.5 The Mutual Fund Finder page helps you find information about mutual funds.

Figure 19.6 The Mutual Fund Finder page has several standard searches to make finding mutual funds easier.

Figure 19.7 This window shows the results of a mutual fund search.

Choosing a Mutual Fund

Thousands of mutual funds are available, and each fund has its own investment objectives. Selecting a mutual fund that meets your criteria for investment is fairly easy using Quicken.com, because it contains detailed information on almost all funds.

To find a mutual fund:

1. From the Quicken.com home page (shown in **Figure 19.1**), click "Pick Top Funds" from the "Top Features" section at the upper left. The Mutual Fund Finder page (**Figure 19.5**) appears.

2. Click the "Popular Searches" link.
   A list of canned (but still useful) searches appears (**Figure 19.6**).

3. Click on a type of search that interests you. The Mutual Fund Finder will show the results of your search (**Figure 19.7**). (For example, clicking "Ranked by 5 year Performance" will show you a ranking of the mutual fund against other funds.)

(continued)

CHOOSING A MUTUAL FUND

4. To refine your search, change the variables listed above the chart in the Display and Sort pull-down menus, or click the EasyStep Search wizard link to go step by step through a more customized process. Or you can make a more sophisticated search by clicking the Full Search link on the left.

✔ Tip

■ You can find more information on mutual funds by clicking Funds on the navigation bar across the top of most screens to open the Mutual Funds page (**Figure 19.8**).

Figure 19.8 The Mutual Funds page has additional information and tools to help you choose a fund that's right for you.

Figure 19.9 Use the navigation bar on the main Investing Basics page to get quick answers to your questions.

Figure 19.10 Find the question that you want answered in the QuickAnswers list.

Insights on Investing

Investing can be confusing. The terminology is often complex, with arcane concepts, weird acronyms, and convoluted explanations. Do you know what an index fund is? Why is Morningstar important? What does it mean to sell a stock short? Are DRIPs good for you? Thankfully, Quicken.com has a place where you can find answers to your questions.

To get answers to basic investing questions:

1. From the Quicken.com home page, click Investments in the left-hand column to open the Investments page. Then click Basics under the Departments heading on the left.

   The Investing Basics page appears (**Figure 19.9**).

2. In the navigation bar on the left side of the page, click "QuickAnswers" to open QuickAnswers page (**Figure 19.10**).

3. Find the question that you want answered in the QuickAnswers list, and then click the question to jump to its answer page. If you can't find the question that you want answered in the list, look through the Related Links navigation bar on the left side of the page for a section of the site that might help you.

INSIGHTS ON INVESTING

Getting Tax Information

The more information you have about taxes, the more likely you are to make intelligent decisions when tax time comes. The Taxes section of Quicken.com has a lot of general tax information and a tax estimating tool—and you can even download federal and state tax forms from the site.

To find tax tips and advice:

1. From the main Quicken.com page (shown in **Figure 19.1**), scroll down the list on the left and click Taxes.

   The main Taxes page appears (**Figure 19.11**).

2. On the right side of the page, under the heading entitled "Tax Topics", find the category of information that you need, and then click it to jump to an information page.

Figure 19.11 Find the category of information that you need from the main Taxes page.

Figure 19.12 Click the name of a Federal tax form to download it from this IRS page.

Downloading tax forms

Quicken.com lets you download federal and state tax forms from the Internal Revenue Service and state revenue office Web sites. You can then print these forms and use them to file your taxes. The files are in a variety of formats, depending on the sites they come from, but Adobe Acrobat format (sometimes called PDF files, for Portable Document Format) is the best one for Mac users. To read Acrobat files, you need to install the free Acrobat Reader program. It comes on the Quicken Deluxe 2000 CD-ROM, it's available on the Quicken.com Web site, or you can download it from Adobe's Web site at http://www.adobe.com.

To download tax forms:

1. In the navigation bar on the left side of the main Taxes page (shown in **Figure 19.11**), click the link "Federal Forms."

   The Retrieve Forms and Instructions page on the Internal Revenue Service site appears (**Figure 19.12**).

2. Scroll down the list until you find the tax form or forms that you want to download. Click the title of a form to download it to your hard disk.

GETTING TAX INFORMATION

Finding Low-Rate Credit Cards

Credit cards are handy to use, but they can be a major source of financial frivolity. If you don't pay off your credit card balance in full every month, you rack up interest charges. If you can't avoid carrying a balance, you can at least try to minimize the amount of interest you're paying by finding a credit card with a low interest rate.

Quicken.com's "Banking & Borrowing" area offers a list of credit card providers with the lowest rates as well as other useful information, such as mortgage interest rates, savings account interest yields, and general banking information.

To find low-rate credit cards:

1. From the main Quicken.com page, choose "Banking & Credit" from the navigation bar on the left.

   The main Banking & Credit page appears (**Figure 19.13**).

2. Click on Credit Cards from the navigation bar. The Credit Card page appears (**Figure 19.14**).

Figure 19.13 In the navigation bar on the left side of this page, click "Credit Cards" under the Banking Topics heading.

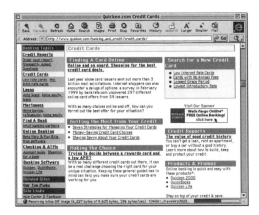

Figure 19.14 Select one of the searches in the box on the right.

Figure 19.15 The results screen shows a selection of credit cards that are ranked according to your criteria.

Figure 19.16 You can find other interest rate information by choosing options from the pull-down menus.

3. Click on "Low Interest Rate Cards" (or one of the other choices) under the "Search for a New Credit Card" heading on the right side of the page.

The results screen appears (**Figure 19.15**), showing credit card companies ranked by the parameter you chose.

✔ Tip

■ From the results screen, you can change your search criteria using the pull down menus above the list. You can even make quick searches for other interest rates, choosing from the options in the pull-down menus that appear for the rate type you have selected. For example, **Figure 19.16** shows how you can get rates for four-year automobile loans in Louisville, Kentucky.

FINDING LOW-RATE CREDIT CARDS

Other Areas of Interest

Each of the 10 departments on the Quicken.com site has its own wealth of information. (It also has, as you have probably noticed, quite a bit of advertising.)

The Life Events department (**Figure 19.17**) focuses on some of the big-ticket items in many of our lives, such as College, Weddings, Parenting, Travel, and Retirement.

The Saving & Spending department (**Figure 19.18**) is sort a catch-all for good economic advice.

The Message Boards area (**Figure 19.19**) is a collection of wide-ranging forums on stocks, insurance, and other issues; from here you can read what other people have to say about these issues and add comments of your own.

In general, you will find that Quicken.com and all the links it provides are about as rich a resource for economic advice and research as you are likely to find without paying for it.

Figure 19.17 The Life Events screen helps you plan for life's big expenditures.

Figure 19.18 The Saving and Spending department tells you lots of things you probably should already know.

Figure 19.19 In the Message Boards, there is a free-flowing exchange of information, misinformation and gossip for you to sort through.

INDEX

A

About Quicken Help, 12
account buttons, 7
account registers. *See* registers
accounts. *See also individual accounts*
  for assets, 18, 132
  balancing, 79–84
  creating, 19
  current status of, 73
  deleting, 20
  description of, 15
  editing, 20
  enabling for online use, 96
  entering opening balances, 19
  hiding vs. deleting, 20
  maximum number of, 15
  printing list of, 114
  registers for, 31–46
  setting up, 15–20
  transferring money between, 40–42
  types of, 18
Accounts, Insights page, 73
Accounts window, 19
Acrobat Reader, tax forms and, 185
Action Plan (Retirement Planner), 159
Action Plan window, 163
Action Type window, 137
Actions button, 147
activity areas, 5
Add Page Break icon, 109
Add Security button, 136
Add Security dialog box, 137
Adjust Ending Balance window, 84
Adjust Register button, 84
alignment, check printing, 58
amortized loans, 123
applications included with Quicken Deluxe, 14
Asset accounts, 18, 132
Assets & Debt area, 5
Assets worksheet, 157

Assign Tax Links window, 26
ATM withdrawals, 35, 99
automatic operations
  data file backup, 10
  entering check numbers, 33
  saving work, 4
  updating of QuickFill list, 48

B

backdrop, 6, 8
backing up data file, 4, 10
Balance column, 34
balances
  adjusting, 84
  opening, 19
  problems with, 81
balancing accounts, 79–84
  adjusting ending balance, 84
  checking accounts, 80–81
  correcting transaction errors, 81, 83, 84
  credit card accounts, 82
  money market accounts, 80–81
  savings accounts, 80–81
Balloon Help, 12
Bank accounts, 18
Bank button, 16, 17
Banking area, 5
banking online, 93–102
bar graphs, 73, 74, 76, 92
Beginning Balance box, 80
Billminder, 61, 70
bills, paying online, 93, 100–102
borrowing money, 123, 124–126
browsers, 94, 178, 179
Budget Monitor, 92
Budget Monitoring window, 92
Budget Setup window, 91
Budgeting function, 90–91
budgets
  Budget Monitor, 92
  Budgeting function, 90–91
  controlling debt with, 90–92

budgets *(continued)*
  current status of, 73
  Debt Reduction Planner, 14, 77, 154, 160–163
  QuickBudget option, 90
  setting up, 90–91
Budgets, Insights page, 73
Business check box, 16
buttons, 7, 9. *See also individual buttons*
Buy dialog box, 138
buying securities, 146–147

C

calculator icon, 54
calculators
  financial planning calculators, 167
  Investment Calculator, 167
  Quicken Tax Planner, 170
  QuickMath, 45
  Refinance calculator, xiv
Calendar, 61–70
  adding scheduled transactions, 62–64
  deleting transactions, 65–66
  description of, 61
  displaying, 62
  editing transactions in, 65
  notes, 69
  Scheduled Transactions section and, 74
  viewing transactions in, 65
calendar icon, 32
Capital Gains reports, 174, 175
Cash accounts, 18
categories
  assigning to transactions, 22–23, 33
  benefits of, 21
  creating, 23
  customizing, 22–25
  deleting, 25
  description of, 16, 21
  dividing transactions among, 36

INDEX